WHAT EVERY
TEENAGER *REALLY*
WANTS TO KNOW
ABOUT SEX

WHAT EVERY TEENAGER *REALLY* WANTS TO KNOW ABOUT SEX

With the Startling New Information Every Parent Should Read

Dr. Sylvia S. Hacker

With Randi Hacker

Carroll & Graf Publishers, Inc.
New York

First Carroll & Graf edition 1993

Carroll & Graf Publishers, Inc.
260 Fifth Avenue
New York, NY 10001

Library of Congress Cataloging-in-Publication Data

Hacker, Sylvia.
    What every teenager really wants to know about sex : with
the startling new information every parent should read / Sylvia
Hacker, with Randi Hacker.
        p.   cm.
    ISBN 0-88184-969-3 : $10.95
    1. Sex instruction for teenagers. 2. Teenagers—Sexual
behavior. I. Hacker, Randi. II. Title.
HQ35.H33 1993
306.7′0835—dc20   93-8505
                                                           CIP

Manufactured in the United States of America

I want to thank my friend and daughter Randi for helping me write this book. I treasure the fact that communications have always been open between us.

Acknowledgments

First of all, thanks to my friend, author Tom Connellan, who, upon hearing my lectures, persistently urged me to write a book. I was further encouraged by my various audiences of parents, professionals, and students, who kept shouting, "Where's the book?"

I thank all those who critiqued my original "academic" manuscript, and who gave me important feedback on how it read and which ideas might be clarified: university experts on genetics; my two wonderful daughters Randi and Pam; my dear sister Sonya; my friends and colleagues—famous author Sol Gordon and fellow teacher Judith Heath; —and my agent Jim Levine.

Thank you also to Steven Merino who often typed the additions and changes in the original manuscript, and to my talented friend, attorney Elizabeth Schwartz, who offered invaluable legal advice.

I am delighted that my daughter Randi, who is (not because I'm her mother) a wonderful free-lance writer, was able to free up her time to whip the book into this final form. I treasure the fact that she is my friend and someone with whom I've had open and honest communication.

Contents

Contents

Introduction

As a sex educator, I spend a lot of time talking to teens in junior and senior high schools. After some initial embarrassment and giggling over the subject matter, the kids settle down and get into discussion of this usually taboo subject. They ask me questions. They give me answers. Their interest and innocence about sex is far reaching.

When their parents ask what we talk about, they are often shocked to hear how much their children know—and don't know—about sexuality, and how much they, as parents, don't know about what their kids are doing sexually. Today parents can't afford to be ignorant of their children's sexual activity. And teens themselves can't afford to be sexually active, guided by myth and misinformation.

Teenagers are sexual beings. We all are from birth. To deny this is to deny our own nature and put ourselves—and our children—at risk. AIDS and other sexually transmitted diseases are dangers of uninformed sexual behavior. Whether we, as parents, want our children to engage in sex or not isn't the point. They *are* exploring sexuality. They can do so in an informed way and be safe, or in an uninformed way, and be at risk.

If you are a parent, this book will help you understand what your teenage child is going through as he or she discovers the pleasures of sexual interaction. It will help you help your teen move through this phase in a safe, responsible, and healthy way. It will help you stay calm during what can be a turbulent emotional time for you and your child. And it will help you stay in touch with your child at a time when he or she starts shutting you out during the characteristic adolescent quest for independence.

When you have finished reading this book, leave it in your teen's room. By flipping through it and reading the answers to questions posed by kids their own ages, your child will learn that he or she is not alone in questioning what is going on. Your child will learn how to act responsibly and take care of himself or herself while still enjoying the excitement of sexual awakening. Any kid from age 12 through age 18 will find answers, reassurances, and important information in this book.

If you are a teenager, you can skip the first two chapters—they're for your parents—and go straight to page 35. You don't have to read this book word for word. Flip around. Focus on a subject that interests you. Read a couple of questions here and there. Show the book to your friends. You'll learn a thing or two about sexuality, and I can guarantee that you won't be bored.

Part One:
What Parents Need to Know

Letter to Parents

Dear Parent,

Things have changed since you were a kid. In those days, teens definitely had sex, but not nearly as many did, and certainly not as openly. The moral taboos against teen sex were stronger then. While those taboos are still given lip service today, the prohibition isn't felt as keenly. Today's teens aren't asking "Should we have sex?" They're asking "When [on which date] *will* we have sex?"

As parents, that means you have something to worry about. Not that your teens are sexual—that's normal. But that your kids are engaging in sex without understanding the ramifications of their actions. I'm not just talking about reputation and unwanted pregnancy. The risks of teen sex today are far more dangerous than they have ever been. AIDS and other sexually transmitted diseases make irresponsible sex a health hazard.

How did all this happen? There's a lot of blaming going around, but if you look at our sexual history, you will realize that no one is to blame for all these changes. Chapter 1 will acquaint you with the historical perspective and teach you why blaming doesn't get you anywhere.

Rather than try to prevent kids from acting sexual—a pretty unsuccessful tactic, to judge from experience—I propose another, more realistic solution: Work with your kids to teach them a healthy new way to approach and act on their own sexuality—an approach that not only keeps them safe, but prepares them for a rich, satisfying sex life once they have grown up.

This book is designed to help you help your teens—and yourself—get through the hormone-intensive, extreme teen years alive, well, and on speaking terms with each another. They have to learn about alternatives to intercourse, i.e., behaviors that I call collectively "outercourse."

They also have to learn thoroughly, just in case they *do* have intercourse, how to use a condom effectively. Read on!

Sincerely,

Sylvia Hacker

Chapter 1
From Intercourse to Outercourse:
The Pleasuring Alternative

Whether you choose to accept it or not, American teenagers are "doing it." And if they're not doing it, they're *thinking* about doing it. *Your* teens are no exception.

Faced with the inevitability of this hormone-induced sexual state, many people preach abstinence. You yourself might feel this is the best course of action. The question I ask is "Abstinence from what?"

While intercourse is definitely a high-risk sexual behavior, and I recommend abstaining from it, other sexual outlets can be enjoyed. Teenagers have raging hormones and must have some sort of outlet. That's why I believe we can't tell our teens to stop *feeling* sexual. What we *can* tell them is how to channel their sexual *behavior* in healthy, responsible ways. Abstinence has to be redefined.

When I talk to teen groups all over the country, I tell them there are alternatives that are just as much fun and usually even more pleasurable than intercourse. I call these activities "outercourse." They're safe and they're satisfying. My message to teens everywhere is to abstain from intercourse, *not* from sexuality. I have found, through the years, that teens are extremely open to these alternatives because their pleasure-seeking potential is high and their hormones are active. What's more, one of the leading characteristics of teenagers is their poor reaction to the lack of choice. As one boy said to me at one of my talks, "You know, if they tell us not to do something, we're gonna do it." Given alternatives, teens tend to choose something that will please them and yet will mollify their parents.

The focus of my talks is sexual enjoyment with an emphasis on responsibility, safety, love, respect, and commitment. In addition, I stress an element that is, by and large, left out of other talks about sexuality: that it's fun. I tell teens, "There's nothing wrong with feeling good." Please understand that I am certainly not a proponent of unbridled pleasure seeking! But what's wrong with pleasure *if* it's attained safely and responsibly? I urge them to celebrate and honor their own sexuality so that they won't let other people—or themselves—tamper with or devalue this treasured possession. If they can engage in fun, safe, and responsible sex, they won't need to turn to alcohol and drugs to avoid confronting their real feelings.

Over the years, I have reviewed a number of recommended sexuality curricula and have found that they are fear-based and disparaging toward sexuality. My approach differs in that I acknowledge and accept human sexuality and view it in a healthy, joyful way.

Teens today are engaging in sexual play. They feel compelled to. They are experiencing new and exciting feelings as a result of the release of hormones into their bloodstreams. Their sexual curiosity is a natural outgrowth of the maturation process.

Unfortunately, our country's attitude about sexuality is not maturing as quickly as teens are. Sex education in this country—when it's taught —is sketchy and ineffective. It's mostly what I call an "organ recital": a total focus on the organs of reproduction, with a little physiology thrown in. Even when contraception is taught, it is often done in the context of dire warnings about its huge failure rate. Unfortunately, many of the statistics cited in school programs such as "Sex Respect" (which teaches abstinence) and others, are incorrect and are not documented. As a result, the American teen pregnancy rate is twice as high as that of any other industrialized nation. As the research from the noted Guttmacher Institute concluded, "In those other countries, they're trying to wipe out teen pregnancy. In this country, we're trying to wipe out teen sexuality."

One of the reasons we are so behind in the sex education area is that we're still stuck between the old sexual morality and a quest for sexual freedom. Prior to World War II, the old sexual norm in our society might have been summarized briefly as follows:

Sex is bad, except in marriage (and then you shouldn't enjoy it too much, especially if you're a woman), but parenthood is good.

You can see that sex, under this norm, was meant primarily for procreation. Pleasure was taboo. Most anything to do with pleasure was considered deviant, aberrant and, of course, immoral. There were three major premises under this norm:

1. Sex = intercourse only.
2. Children and the elderly are asexual.

3. Sexual thoughts, feelings, and fantasies are equally as evil as sexual deeds.

Let me elaborate a bit on each of these:

1. Sex = intercourse only.

If the purpose of sex is only to make babies, we must not dwell on the frills lest we get carried away. As someone in one of my audiences once said, "Boy, it would have been easy to write a sex manual in those days. You would need only two sentences: Thrust in and out. Repeat if necessary."

2. Children and the elderly are asexual.

Despite evidence to the contrary, anyone for whom reproduction was considered unneeded or inappropriate was simply not supposed to have sexual feelings. And a lot of effort was put into keeping it that way. Kids were warned of dire consequences for touching their genitals, and the elderly were dubbed "dirty old men and women" if they showed any lingering interest in sexual activity.

3. Sexual thoughts, feelings, and fantasies are equally as evil as sexual deeds.

Since sex was bad and dirty, people (especially women) were enjoined to rid themselves of sexual thoughts—to sublimate them and think of nobler things instead. To keep minds and hands busy, boys were encouraged to engage in sports and cold showers. Girls were taught to read a lot, do household chores, and to mend and embroider. If boys defied the norm, the attitude was "Boys will be boys." But for girls, there existed the "madonna/whore" complex. Men married madonnas and had sex with whores. A woman who enjoyed sex and didn't feel guilty was rendered virtually unmarriageable. It was clearly a man's world.

In those days, sex was the trading commodity for marriage. Men pledged "love" to get sex, and women promised sex to get "love"—the word "love" meaning to "take care of" and to "be taken care of," respectively. The advantages for the man, as the exclusive breadwinner and head of the household, were economic power and status, and a mate *exclusively* his. The advantage of keeping women pure and virginal meant that men had power sexually, too. They didn't have to be great lovers. They didn't have to please their wives sexually. Obviously, virgins can't make comparisons.

The advantage for women was financial security all their lives. However, the disadvantages for women were great. A woman was not encouraged to develop her talents or abilities. Instead, she had to submerge her identity to promote her husband's development.

As a result of World War II, in which women entered the workplace in record numbers, some major socioeconomic changes occurred. In order to understand them, let's look at the Hierarchy of Needs theory conceived by Abraham Maslow, a famous twentieth-century psychologist. Maslow's hierarchy states that human beings have different levels of needs, and that each level must be satisfied before progress can be made to the next level. The most basic level consists of the physiological needs: food, clothing and shelter. Without these three, there can be no survival.

Once these survival needs are met, people can turn to the next level: security, safety, and a sense of belonging.

After this need level is satisfied, individuals can go on to explore a succession of ego needs that focus on "Who am I?" and "What can I become?" At the top of the hierarchy—and far removed from survival needs—is self-actualization: achieving all you are capable of becoming.

Before World War II, most Americans were essentially operating at Maslow's lowest level: working hard just to eke out a living for their families. After World War II, the United States prospered. Material goods were produced in abundance, and everyone was working. A new, affluent middle class was created. More survival and security needs were being met by more people, so they could turn their attention to ego needs for themselves and their children. Therefore, in the atmosphere of looking toward a bright future, they proceeded to give birth to lots of children: the baby-boom generation.

By the 1960s, the exceptionally-nurtured baby boomers, reared to focus on ego needs, became the self-obsessed "me" generation who cried, "I'm gonna do my own thing!" For this generation, there existed an unparalleled sense of hope and freedom of choice. They questioned and rebelled against all of society's old rules and regulations, including the ones about sex. In fact, since sex is such a strong drive, it's not surprising that those rules were among the first to go. Young people could not see any advantage to delaying gratification. Sexual exploration was as much a part of this era as love-ins, communes, and unisex dorms.

This atmosphere of freedom greatly affected women. The war had already given them a taste of liberation, and later developments in contraception furthered their sexual liberation. The advent of the pill gave women a revolutionary perception of sexual freedom. It potentially made available to them some of the power and fun that earlier had been reserved for men.

But because of our ignorance about sexuality, and the rapid advance of the sexual revolution, we failed to take time out to see what kind of sex education was needed to keep up with the changes. Thus, although the old norm began to erode and behavior was changing, old attitudes lingered. Young people were trying sexual intercourse and, although they knew that the pill (and other methods) were available, they were still too guilty and ashamed to use protection. Consequently, the seventies saw the repercussions of sexual freedom without sexual guidance. Teen pregnancy rates soared. Gonorrhea reached epidemic proportions. New sexually transmitted diseases, such as genital warts, herpes, and chlamydia, appeared. Today, our teen pregnancy rate is still sky-high and a more terrifying STD—AIDS —is making intercourse one of the riskiest activities people can engage in.

Here in the nineties, we're working hard to regain our equilibrium in many areas: economically, racially, and environmentally. We must also work on our attitudes toward sexuality. The abstinence preached and mostly practiced in an earlier time is no longer working. We are in transition without new norms. No wonder we're in a state of confusion!

The kind of sex education introduced in recent years has been a failure. Because of our persistent discomfort about sexuality, those courses labeled "Sex Education" are merely courses in internal plumbing. Sol Gordon, a noted contemporary sex educator, calls it "the relentless pursuit of the fallopian tubes." When I was growing up, before

World War II, I knew nothing about sexuality. But I knew I didn't know. Now, because kids have had some kind of sexuality course, they think they know, but they don't. Of the hundreds and hundreds of questions I have accumulated from teens over the years, there is not one on the fallopian tubes—nor on the epididymis or vas deferens. (two male reproductive structures). While some new curricula are being introduced that include methods of contraception, they still emphasize the antisexual, antipleasure attitudes of the old norm.

The answer is not to deny the sexuality of our teens, but instead to acknowledge it and teach them ways to be sexual without endangering themselves. It's up to us as parents to help our teens be sexual and responsible. Instead of just saying no to sexuality, our teens have to say "know" to sexuality.

Chapter 2
Just Say <u>KNOW</u> (Or, Knowledge Equals Safety: More on <u>Outercourse</u>)

N ow that I have presented the argument that teens everywhere are sexual beings exploring pleasuring, it's time to discuss the best way to guide them in this activity.

At this time, teens are rushing headlong into sexual intercourse. This behavior is dangerous for many reasons. First, there's the problem of unwanted pregnancy. Second, there's the risk of contracting one of the many sexually transmitted diseases that are epidemic, including AIDS, which is lethal.

Intercourse is also unsatisfying for many teens —especially girls. Most teenage girls admit that sex is not as much fun for them as it is for their boyfriends. But peer pressure, the desire to be loved, and the ignorance of other pleasuring techniques, makes intercourse the only route they can take. In our society, even in 1993, sex still equals intercourse only—shades of the old restrictive norm. However, we now know, from a great deal of research, that intercourse is highly overrated when it comes to mutual enjoyment.

Teens are moving inevitably into intercourse because there is simply no information available on pleasuring alternatives. Pleasuring—bringing a partner to orgasm without intercourse—is something that our teens need to learn. They need to understand and be proud of the fact that they are sexual beings and that there are multiple sexual activities they can engage in and enjoy. And, parents, don't be jealous. You can learn some of these techniques, too. I believe that if we considered our sexuality wonderful, something to celebrate, we wouldn't let so much harm come to such a prized possession!

In order for our teens to be comfortable with their sexuality, they've got to be taught the facts about *sexuality*, and not just reproduction. We, as a society, have to develop a new Norm of Acknowledgment that we are pleasure-seeking sexual beings. Under such a norm, three major premises are:

1. Sexuality is far more than intercourse.
2. Children and elderly people are sexual.
3. All thoughts, feelings, and fantasies are normal. It's the behavior that needs to be monitored and disciplined.

Let me elaborate on each of these:

1. Sexuality is far more than intercourse.

First, we must become comfortable with penises, vaginas, and semen. We have to learn about the wonderful and most remarkable mechanisms that go into erections and lubrication. We have to talk about, and truly appreciate the metabolic sexual by-products of our bodies, such as semen and vaginal moisture. We have to learn more about masturbation, mutual masturbation, oral and anal sex, and homosexuality. We have to be able to think of these activities as pleasurable, exciting and, above all, normal. In our society, these activities are still considered deviant. This means that they are still done clandestinely, with shame and guilt instead of comfort.

This discomfort also promotes teenagers' huge interest in these pleasuring activities. When a subject is taboo, it immediately becomes intriguing, especially among teens who are exploring and rebelling and trying out new things. Teens are intensely curious about sexuality. Denying that they are doesn't help. Twelve-year-olds ask me, "What's sixty-nine?" "What's a blowjob?" "Why is it called 'going down'?" We need to examine all the sexual activities that human beings engage in, no matter how embarrassing it may be at first, so that we can ask, "Is this activity OK or not OK, and why?"

Unfortunately, the information teens are getting is full of misconceptions and myths. This is because their major source of information is themselves, and they don't know anything because they aren't being taught. There are very few places for kids to get the real facts about sexuality: the facts that deal with emotions, peer pressure, infatuation, love, and risk. Kids are fumbling through their sexual awakening when they could be guided in ways that would be less harmful to them—and more pleasurable. For example, some girls tell me they engage in anal sex—a very high-risk sexual behavior when it comes to AIDS transmission—as a form of birth control. If these girls knew more facts, they would be less likely to engage in such a risky activity without knowing how to protect themselves.

You may think that teaching teens about sexuality will encourage them to have sex. You may think that by teaching them, we are telling them to do it. Not true. They're *already* doing it. But, because they don't know anything, many of them are going straight to intercourse without understanding the risks or being aware of the alternatives. Knowledge about sexuality reduces the chance that teens will engage in early intercourse and other risky behavior. Some very well-designed studies have shown this to be true. Some parents (especially fathers) say that if kids get into pleasuring, it will inevitably end up in intercourse—that I'm naïve to think that a guy can control himself. This perception that men can't control themselves has got to go! It derives from the old norm that "boys will be boys." It is demeaning to men to say that. In my new proposed norm, boys would be taught that they can certainly control themselves. That's part of learning to be an adult. Boys and girls are intelligent creatures and can be trained. We just haven't tried that kind of education yet.

2. Children and the elderly are sexual.

All the data are in on this. We are sexual from womb to tomb. Through ultrasound photography, researchers have even discovered that male fetuses get erections. The last time I said this, a man in one of my audiences responded, "I think we should say, 'We are sexual from the sperm to the worm.' " Whereupon, another person, perhaps more religiously oriented, piped up, "How about saying 'We are sexual from the erection to the resurrection?' "

No matter how we say it, we need to know that babies will discover their genitals early. They will want to touch and rub them because it will be pleasurable. This is normal exploratory behavior. If children are slapped or punished for such behavior, their negative antisex education has been launched! As kids grow and continue their pleasure seeking, we need to acknowledge that touching their genitals feels good, but is a private behavior and must be done only in private. Instead of teaching them not to do it, we must teach children to pick out a place (like their room or the bathroom) where they can go to engage in this normal exploration.

It is especially important for parents of disabled children to teach this because, in the past, the assumption was that they would never find a partner and therefore would be asexual. Not true. For the kids who are mentally impaired in any way, acknowledgment that masturbation feels good—but is private—is extremely important. It might be the only sexual outlet in their lives, and it is a very satisfying one for releasing normal sexual tension—tension that otherwise may be released in acting out. The difference involved in teaching these youngsters is that the message needs to be repeated many times until it is absorbed. A mother of an autistic boy recently told me that the whole family (she, her husband, and two other sons) has cooperated in getting this message across to the boy. Not only has it been successful for the boy (who is now a teenager), but it is calmly accepted as part of the family dynamic. What a good learning experience for everyone!

We also know that older men and women who have enjoyed their sexuality throughout their lives will continue to enjoy it into old age. Even when the body slows up (as it inevitably will in all ways), and erections, lubrication, and orgasms are not as frequent or as strong, there is still joy in kissing, caressing, and mutual sex play of all sorts. The pleasure is the same, and often better, when the focus is taken off intercourse. For the single elderly, just as for any single person, masturbation—or, as I like to call it, fantasy and friction—is a great outlet.

As parents, you play a key role in the healthy attitude your kids can have about sex and sexuality. Research shows that parents who create a climate in which they can talk about sexuality with their children as they grow up and an atmosphere in which questions are encouraged and straight answers are given, have teens who are less likely to dash into intercourse. When these teens do become sexually active, they tend to use contraception more than young people who have come from homes where sex is not discussed.

Schools can help, too. When a school acknowledges the sexuality of its students, it implies community acknowledgment as well. This attitude helps teens become more comfortable with their own sexuality. Some school-based clinics have slashed teen pregnancy rates by a whopping 66 percent.

3. Sexual thoughts, feelings and fantasies are normal. It's the behavior that needs monitoring and discipline.

This concept represents the essence of morality because it addresses how we treat each other as fellow human beings. We can think, feel, and fantasize anything we want to—that's human and normal. But we may not *do* everything we want to. The definition of an adult is someone who knows which thoughts, emotions, and daydreams are OK to act on and which aren't. Once, in a high school, when I talked about just that, a boy asked me confrontationally, "Based on what?" "Based on nonexploitation" was my reply.

And this nonexploitation criterion is of the utmost importance. We may feel angry at someone and fantasize about getting even—maybe dumping a load of garbage on their front lawn. Or we might actively dislike or strongly disagree with someone and wish we could just get rid of him. However, if we are grown-ups, we don't act on these thoughts or feelings. That's part of what it means to be a moral individual. It refers to all behavior, not only sexual.

It is essential to get the morality/grown-up concept across to young people early. Take the issues of rape and incest, for example. Sexual arousal is very normal in dating, where two people are attracted to each other. Very often the arousal leads to heavy "making out": necking, petting, removal of items of clothing and so forth. However, even if the boy has an enormous erection and is thinking "INTERCOURSE," if the girl says, "I don't think I want to go all the way," a boy who is trained to be a *grown-up* will stop. Even in families, sexual feelings toward each other are normal, but grown-ups do not act on them. See the chapter on rape and incest for further information about this topic.

In today's society, people are seeking self-gratification and are pushing the limits to their own and others' detriment. The "I'm gonna do my own thing" mentality of the sixties has gotten out of control. We haven't been offering adequate education on these moral and ethical issues because we haven't yet crystallized new norms. As a result, in the area of sexuality, we are scared and disgusted. We tend to blame and want to censor. Understandably, this mood has escalated because of the rising incidence of AIDS. But it is not the inherent, normal sexual feelings, thoughts, and fantasies we should be blaming. It's the irresponsible and exploitive behaviors we must train kids against!

Sex education and contraceptive availability begin very early in other industrialized nations. That's why the teen pregnancy rate in the Netherlands is roughly 15 percent of ours, followed closely by Sweden and Denmark. At the same time, there is no evidence of any breakdown in family values in these countries—something many in this country cry will happen if we teach our kids about sex and sexuality. It has also been shown that kids in those countries are no more sexually active than kids in ours. Surely we can learn something from these statistics.

The most important thing we can do is teach adolescents to explore their bodies safely and responsibly in ways that don't put them or their partners at risk. We can do that by taking the shame out of sexuality. We can validate masturbation—it's a wonderful and safe way to relieve sexual tension, and it helps kids find out what excites them so that they can tell future partners how to give them the greatest pleasure. That's one of the secrets of a satisfying sex life. It's also one of the concepts of "outercourse": deriving pleasure without intercourse.

We must also teach young people about alternative ways of pleasuring each other. Research confirms that orgasms without vaginal penetration

26

can be far more intense. This is a safe and satisfying alternative to intercourse.

Outercourse also includes anal and oral stimulation, which can be done safely and responsibly, without penetration, as long as we learn how to approach them knowledgeably.

Don't forget, though, that it isn't *mandatory* that the above techniques be practiced. Abstinence is a viable alternative, but it is crucial that we learn about all the alternatives in order to make informed choices, rather than persisting in thinking that intercourse is the ultimate prize.

When I talk about outercourse with teens, girls cheer. Most girls engage in intercourse because they are afraid of losing their boyfriends. They also hope that it is going to be as exciting as their fantasies lead them to think. But as many as 80 percent of girls don't have an orgasm when they first start having sex. They love the idea of alternatives that might be more pleasurable and less risky. For the first time in their lives, they have a legitimate way to abstain from intercourse—lowering the danger of unwanted pregnancy and STD transmission—while satisfying themselves and their boyfriends. Using pleasuring alternatives, girls can be sexy and safe. And, despite the old outmoded messages, girls are very interested in sexual pleasure!

Boys will pay attention when I tell them how they can experience maximum pleasure and be great lovers without intercourse. When I call my talk "How to Be a Great Lover," boys show up. With any other title, I end up mostly with girls. Just recently a teenage boy, who had confessed to me after one of my talks, that his girlfriend never had orgasms, later asked his high-school counselor to call me and tell me that he had finally gotten his partner to have an orgasm without intercourse! He was so proud of himself that I hope he communicates his discovery to all his male friends!

Naturally, it won't be easy for all parents to adopt a comfortable approach to sexuality. Our society still makes it difficult to do so. Still, there are ways that you, as parents, can help your teen enter the sexually intense years equipped with knowledge that will help them stay safe. Here are a few tips on how to make sexual conversation comfortable:

1. **Be honest.** We need to recognize that, despite our scientific knowledge about the advantages of masturbation, there are a number of people who don't believe in it for religious reasons. It is certainly their choice not to engage in it, and we must respect different values. That's why I say "Masturbation is normal whether you do it or not." But we may not lie to our kids to get them not to do it. Long ago, we used to tell young people—and even doctors would say it—that masturbation caused you to go blind, grow hair on your palms, or end up in an insane asylum. We now know for certain these are myths. If parents are

against masturbation, they must tell their kids, "In our value system, masturbation is not OK. However, not everyone feels that way." This will enable kids to recognize that there is a multiplicity of values in the world. If the parent lies, when the kids go out into the world and observe other kids masturbating without harmful consequences, they will lose faith in their parents.

2. **Be open with your kids.** Don't be afraid to tell them you're afraid they will become pregnant or get sick. Discuss with them the reasons why intercourse might not be a good idea and the alternatives. This includes not only outercourse, but total abstinence as well. During discussions like this, be prepared for your kids to ask you about your sexual activities. Younger kids, when they're taught about sexuality, even ask if they can watch you "do it." You must appeal to their sense of privacy. After all, sexual behavior is private, and you wouldn't ask them about their private behavior! Just let them know that you can get books (or even anatomically correct dolls) for them to learn from. However, *do* indicate that you are a sexual person, and that sex is a beautiful part of life.

3. **Admit that you're embarrassed, if you are.** Also admit it if you don't know the answers to some questions. After all, how many people in this country are really comfortable or knowledgeable about sexuality? Your kid might be embarrassed, too. The only way to get comfortable is to

talk about it. And, if you admit your discomfort or lack of knowledge, it often enables your child to say, "OK, Mom [or Dad], I'll find out for us!" It's wonderful to say to kids, "Let's learn together." Then you have established an atmosphere for communication.

4. **Accept that your teen is thinking about—and possibly engaging in—sexual activities.** Once you have faced that, you can start to handle the reality responsibly. If they are having sex, you can talk to them about the safest way to do so. To pretend they're not having sex—or at least thinking about it—only puts up a barrier between you and your child.

5. **Talk about morality with your kids.** Is it moral to pretend that sex doesn't exist until an unwanted pregnancy shows up? Or is it moral to acknowledge sexuality and prevent an unwanted pregnancy? Morality involves much more than just sexuality. It includes how we treat each other as human beings in all areas.

6. **Believe that sexuality is a healthy part of growing up.** You were once a teen. You remember your own raging hormones and how distressing it was to suppress them and be secretive about the whole process. Think how much healthier your children can be if they accept their sexuality as a normal part of life. Ask yourself "What's the trade-off?" Isn't it better to allow your kids to become sexually active safely and responsibly, than to risk pregnancy and disease?

7. **Don't be discouraged.** Some parents have told me that when they try to bring up the subject of sexuality, their teenager will suddenly say, "I just remembered—I have homework to do." Most teens are protective of their personal life, especially when the subject has not been discussed much at home in the past. So, I sometimes say jokingly, "If you want your kids to do homework, just start asking them about their sex lives." If at first you can't convince them to talk with you, even if you tell them you love them, are worried, or need to learn something yourself, then some strategies might have to be employed. For example, if you have a partner, conspire with him or her to talk about a subject of concern when the whole family is at dinner one night. Talk only to each other. Don't even look at the kids. Don't ask them for comments. Just bring up all the issues you are worrying about with your partner and, if you don't corner your teens, they'll usually hang around and listen. They might even jump in and add something. This strategy is especially effective if there are younger kids at the table, as well. The younger ones are usually less reluctant to join in, ask questions and make remarks. And don't worry that they're too young to be hearing "that stuff." The earlier the scene is set for being able to bring up questions on sexuality, the better. If you are a single parent, invite an open-minded grownup to dinner and implement the

same plan. I get lots of dinner invitations for that reason, and I've seen the strategy work.

If that particular strategy doesn't work, try leaving various books with provocative titles around the house. Don't tell the kids to read them if they seem resistant to such suggestions. If one of them asks what the book on the coffee table is about, you might say, "It's a book someone recommended to me, but I don't know if you'd want to read it. It has an awful lot of sexual stuff in it." You can be sure it will be looked at!

8. **Ask your children whether they know any other adults they feel comfortable talking about their concerns with.** *You* can even suggest other grownups, if you like. It will help both of you if you can think of someone—a counselor, a friend, a relative, even a teacher—your teen can confide in. It's important for teens to have other grownups they can trust, and it will show your child that you understand that need. What's more, it takes you off the hook for being the sole authority they turn to. The more of a support system kids have, the better it is for them.

9. **Give your kids this book.** If you are having a hard time introducing the subject, this book can give you and your kids a jumping-off point for discussion of pretty much any aspect of sexuality. And it's OK to argue about it. Just keep on listening to each other!

One more thing: Don't worry about your kids

reading this chapter. They'll be glad about the advice if it lets them be in an atmosphere which is open to learning.

Good luck!

Part Two:
What Teenagers Want to Know

Letter to Teens

Dear Teens,

I've traveled all over the world talking to young people about sex and sexuality. After I visit a group, someone usually says to me, "You sure tell it like it is. Everyone always tells us what *not* to do. At least you tell us what *to* do."

That's the point. Knowing what to do can make the difference for you between making a mistake that can ruin your life—unwanted pregnancy or catching a sexually transmitted disease—and just having fun.

This book contains straight talk about sex. It also answers questions teens have asked me over the years. I hope it helps you learn about sexual pleasure without risk. And don't miss Chapter 13, which will give you some suggestions on how to deal with your parents.

Sincerely,

Sylvia Hacker

Chapter 3
What about Pleasure? (Or, How to Be a Great Lover without Intercourse)

Most girls don't have orgasms when they start having sex, and a large number of adult women don't have orgasms through intercourse alone. In fact, when I ask kids, "Why do you have sex?" boys answer, "For pleasure." "Sex is fun! It feels great!" "Wow, what a dumb question!" Girls say, "For love."

Above and beyond the possibility of pregnancy and transmission of disease, intercourse is not the best way for two people to pleasure each other. Research has shown that few girls—less than 20 percent—achieve orgasm strictly through intercourse. Many girls say they love being touched and caressed by their lovers but just don't find intercourse satisfying.

Sometimes girls become defensive and say to me, "You don't have to have an orgasm to enjoy sex!" That's true. Who doesn't love being held, hugged and caressed? But why shouldn't they also enjoy an orgasm the way a guy does? In the past, girls and women often saw a man's pleasuring as much more important than their own. These days, if women want to become mature grown-ups, they need to feel as deserving of orgasm as men do. An interesting piece of research shows that the minority of girls who do enjoy their early sexual encounters, come from homes in which masturbation was considered a legitimate outlet. In addition, their mothers showed pride in their own sexuality.

Many guys think they're great lovers because they have gone to bed with a lot of girls. Quantity doesn't make you a good lover. The quality of your lovemaking is the deciding factor. And the quality is based on the CAR principle. All the world's greatest lovers have practiced the CAR principle.

1. Caring—Great lovers care enough about sexuality to make a conscious, deliberate effort to discover what sexual pleasuring is all about. This means taking time and studying with a sense of anticipation whatever you can about the topic. Caring does not necessarily mean being in love. See Chapter 4 for more about love.

2. Attentiveness—Great lovers are attentive not only to the needs of their own bodies, but to the needs of their lovers' bodies as well. They pay attention to their lovers' reactions and modify what they do to give their lovers—and themselves—maximum pleasure. Attentiveness relies heavily on communication, both verbal and nonverbal. You don't always have to talk out loud; that can be embarrassing. There are ways of moving your body or your lover's hands to indicate nonverbally what you would like.

3. Respect—All great lovers respect both their own and their partners' differences and tastes. They don't do things just for their own pleasure. They don't think about coming and leaving their partners "high and dry." They do not pressure their lovers into doing something they don't want to do, nor do they allow anyone to do things that they don't want done.

At times, when speaking to large groups of teens, I've found there are some who act in a rather antisocial way. They giggle loudly, tell jokes, drop condoms, and try everything they can to disrupt the talk. I stop and say, "That group over there will never be great lovers!" They look miffed and puzzled. "Know why?" I continue. "Because they don't care. They're not paying attention, and they have no respect for other people. But you have one more chance before I leave today." And then I let them in on the CAR principle.

The CAR principle means slowing down and getting to know each other over a period of time. It means building up gradually to orgasm through sexual play without intercourse. This kind of pleasuring can be delicious and very exciting. Even if the relationship does not last—and during the teen years you will have many relationships, as you learn who you are and what you want—you are still learning a mature way to relate to another person sexually. And if intercourse isn't considered the inevitable outcome, you're safer, too. You don't have to worry about pregnancy, and your chances of catching an STD are much smaller.

Both boys and girls need to learn the "secret" of being a great lover by acknowledging themselves as sexual creatures and slowly exploring sex play with a sense of responsibility toward themselves and each other. Here are some questions teens have asked me about orgasm and pleasuring:

Q: What is an orgasm?

A: An orgasm—also called a "climax" and "coming"—is an overwhelmingly pleasurable release of energy that occurs during sexual play, whether with a partner or alone. When both lovers achieve orgasm—especially without engaging in intercourse—that is the sign of a really successful pleasuring relationship.

Incidentally, orgasms don't necessarily have to be simultaneous. There's just as much pleasure if one partner comes before the other—as long as you're both interested in seeing that each *has* maximum pleasure. Also, it isn't essential to have an orgasm *every* time! The idea is to aim for orgasm in a loving, patient way, with pleasure along the way as part of the plan.

Q: How can I get my girlfriend to have an orgasm?

A: First of all, this is a question from a boy who wants to be a great lover. It shows that he cares about his girlfriend's pleasure, wants to be attentive to her needs, and respects her right to enjoy herself sexually. The best way to bring your girlfriend to orgasm is to ask her what makes her feel good or to tell her to show you in nonverbal ways what she likes. Caress her in ways she enjoys. Pay attention to her reactions, so you know if you're exciting her or not. Don't pressure her into having intercourse. In fact the less pressure to have intercourse a guy puts on a girl while remaining touching and loving, the more a girl will be turned on.

Q: Is there more than one kind of orgasm?
Yes, two: male and female. Males achieve orgasm in a very different way from females. When they climax, they ejaculate, and semen, the fluid that carries sperm, is ejected from the body through the penis. When girls have an orgasm, there are lots of wonderful contractions in the vaginal area and sometimes trembling all over the body. Girls lubricate, which means they can get pretty wet. The amount of lubrication can depend on how aroused they are. Also, some women just naturally lubricate more than others. Sometimes, because of fear or lack of readiness, a women might not lubricate. Under such circumstances, intercourse (or even finger penetration), can be painful. This is quite common. Many girls ask or write, "When does it stop hurting?" The answer is when they learn to relax and enjoy themselves.

Because the female orgasm is largely internal, many males (especially those who don't pay close attention) don't know whether their partners have come or not. That's why a lot of women can "fake" it. A male ejaculation, being so visible, can't be faked and is often more dramatic.

Q: Can girls have orgasms?
A: Yes, indeed, but many of them never do because their partners are so focused on intercourse

and climaxing themselves that they don't pay enough attention to the level of pleasure their girlfriends are experiencing. Also, too often, girls do not tell their partners what pleases them. Great lovers make sure that, whatever they do, their partners enjoy it, too.

Q: Is it important for your partner to have an orgasm?
A: Yes. Very important. If you are the only one in your relationship who is having an orgasm, then you're not having much communication, are you? Great lovers are as concerned about their partners' orgasm as they are about their own. In fact, really great lovers get almost as much pleasure from their partners' orgasm as they do from their own. Of course, it isn't necessary to always have an orgasm because, with every lovemaking experience, the situation and surroundings may have different effects on your passion and comfort levels. However, why not try to achieve one as often as you can?

Q: Why do guys have orgasms before girls?
A: Mostly, this is because guys are less inhibited about having orgasms, and about their sexuality in general. In our culture, girls aren't encouraged to be as sexual as guys. This means they have trouble with their own desire for pleasure. That can interfere with achieving orgasm. Also, if girls have intercourse and are not well protected, they

worry about getting pregnant or catching an STD. Worry interferes with letting yourself go and having fun. Guys who pressure their girlfriends into having intercourse are not caring lovers. A guy who respects his girlfriend can bring her to orgasm through caressing and sensual touching of all kinds and will encourage her to show him what pleasures her. Of course, it is also wonderful for him to show *her* what turns *him* on the most.

Q: What are ways you can have an orgasm without having sexual intercourse?
A: There are many, and I call them collectively "outercourse." You can masturbate to orgasm while fantasizing about someone you love or lust over. I call this "fantasy and friction." You can pleasure your partner by touching and caressing the parts of his or her body that are sensitive. Playing with breasts or genitals is one way. Massages are another way. A total body massage is a wonderful way of finding out what gives your partner pleasure. Everyone is different. Some people like face or breast massage best. Some love to have their feet or backs massaged more than anything. Even with genital massage, you'll find different places and different pressures preferred by different people. That's why great lovers take time to explore each other's bodies. It's much more fun and lasts longer than intercourse.

Kissing and hugging help, too. Putting all these together can mean that both you and your partner will achieve orgasm without having to worry about pregnancy or sexually transmitted diseases that can accompany intercourse.

Many studies show that most couples can enjoy the best orgasms by learning certain principles that involve a deliberate focus on pleasuring —exploring together what parts of their bodies respond to sexual stimuli and how they respond best. Masters and Johnson, two famous sex researchers, enjoyed a high success rate in treating couples who had lost interest in each other sexually. Their first step was to postpone intercourse. The partners had to excite each other without thinking about intercourse. They learned to touch and caress each other's bodies in new ways. *Sensual* communication was taught, using both verbal and nonverbal exercises.

Another source of information comes from work done with spine-injured men who had returned from the Vietnam War. Paraplegics and quadriplegics no longer able to have erections worried about their masculinity. A number of doctors worked with these men and their partners to teach them to pleasure each other without focusing on intercourse. They used manual, oral, and anal stimulation and massage to excite each other. The men were able to achieve a sensual and psychological release like orgasm, and their partners claimed that these men were the best lovers they ever had. They discovered that the two largest sex organs in the body are the skin and the brain. When these men learned about their sensuality and used their minds to focus on present pleasuring as well as remembering past pleasuring, they became very successful lovers.

Q: Does a man always have to climax when he has sex?
A: No. But if he doesn't climax, it can sometimes be painful. This is called having "blue balls." This condition subsides eventually, and we know that no guy ever died of an unresolved erection. Some immature guys will coerce a woman to have intercourse by saying that blue balls will kill them. They may really think that's true, but it isn't. A woman has to know that a guy can wait until his erection goes away, that he can engage in fantasy and friction, or that they can both enjoy outercourse and he can have an orgasm that way.

Q: What is the easiest way to make a girl come?
A: Not usually through sexual intercourse alone. Women love being stroked and held and caressed. They want friendship from their boyfriends, loving communication, and a slow, tantalizing buildup to lovemaking. Boys who are deliberate, attentive lovers and who encourage their girlfriends to show them what they enjoy (as well as showing their partners what pleasures them), have no trouble bringing their girlfriends to orgasm. Boys who selfishly have only intercourse in

mind usually indulge in quick and substandard foreplay that is not enjoyed by women.

Q: What is a multiple orgasm?
A: Just what it sounds like: having more than one orgasm in a row. In general, it's not very easy to achieve, although women seem to have a better chance at it than men. After men ejaculate, they usually can't have another orgasm right away. Some women, however, can have one orgasm right after another. That is something lovers can explore together with slow, deliberate attention to lovemaking.

Q: How do you fake an orgasm?
A: Guys can't fake an orgasm because they ejaculate.

It's not that hard for a woman to fake an orgasm. We see enough sex play on TV and in the movies to know the outward signs of orgasm: panting, moaning, groaning and writhing, and then shouting "Yes!" or something like that. (See the fun movie, *When Harry Met Sally* for a brilliant scene.) A more important question is, why do you fake an orgasm? Faking an orgasm implies that you *must* come in order to flatter your partner. Why shouldn't your partner know that you haven't had an orgasm? It would be better, in fact, if your partner did know, so that the two of you could try for mutual pleasure.

Q: Does the penis have to touch the clitoris during intercourse to have an orgasm? How can it if it's in the vagina?

A: Good question. The female pleasuring nerve endings are in the clitoris and around the entrance to the vagina. In order for a woman to achieve orgasm, these nerve endings have to be stimulated directly, and gently. When the penis is in the vagina, indirect stimulation occurs. Some women do achieve orgasm this way, depending on the location of the clitoris or the position the couple assumes during lovemaking. But most women don't experience it, or the orgasm is not as strong as it could be. This is another reason not to engage in intercourse. Beside the danger of unwanted pregnancy, and sexually transmitted diseases, intercourse is not always equally pleasurable for both partners.

Keep the penis out of the vagina, and if it is used even just to stimulate the clitoris, wear a condom to be sure no semen accidentally drips into the vagina. Or use your fingers or tongue for stimulation. Also, if you are a male and using your tongue on the female genitals, use a dental dam—a latex square obtainable at drugstores that effectively covers those areas—to protect against AIDS. Just remember: responsibility and safety! These days, any penetration into any opening, without the proper use of condoms, can be hazardous to your health.

Q: Does a guy feel totally let down if a girl doesn't have an orgasm?
A: A lot of guys tell me they do. If they don't, they're not paying much attention to their partners' pleasure in lovemaking, and they're not great lovers. Great lovers care about whether their partners are enjoying themselves, too. They're not in it just for what they can get out of it. They're also in it for what they can *give.*

Q: Is there something wrong with a girl if she doesn't come?
A: No, of course not. The only thing wrong could be that her partner is not taking the time to make sure they are both getting maximum pleasure, or the girl is not letting her partner know what pleasures her. A girl who makes love—and I don't mean intercourse—with someone who cares about her and someone she cares about, can achieve orgasm.

Q: If, while having sex, you don't talk to your partner or don't have an orgasm, does that mean you are talking yourself into sex, or what?
A: If you're not talking to your partner and you're having intercourse without orgasm, you have to ask yourself why you're doing it. If sex isn't fun, safe, and responsible, there's no point in doing it. Find yourself a partner you can talk to about what you like and don't like, who won't pressure you to have intercourse if you don't want to for *any*

reason, and who cares about whether or not you have an orgasm. Sometimes girls will give in to pressure from guys just to keep a boyfriend. But unless he is a worthwhile, caring person, you're better off alone. That will give you the freedom to look for the right guy and, even more important, the practice to learn how to enjoy being by yourself. It is important, so that you don't settle for just any guy.

Q: What are the signs of an orgasm, and can the man tell a girl is having one?
A: A man who observes his girlfriend, who talks to her and learns what she likes and doesn't like, has the best chance of being able to tell whether she is having an orgasm. If he is still unsure, he can always ask her. Some people say an orgasm is like sneezing—just slower, more dramatic, and more fun. There's a buildup, an explosive letting go of control, and a great feeling of serenity afterward.

Q: If you are unable to climax during sex, how can you help yourself?
A: By first finding out, through self-pleasuring, what really turns your body on. Then, by talking to or showing your partner your special pleasure areas. If the two of you find out what each of you likes, then you'll find ways to bring each other to climax without intercourse. If you still can't climax after talking and exploring, you might con-

sider looking for another sex partner or seeking counseling together with your present one.

Q: Is it possible for a girl the age of 17 to physically have an orgasm?
A: Yes. It's possible for a girl the age of 2 to physically have an orgasm. We humans are a sensual, sexual species from birth to death. We can be turned on by any number of things. If you are 17 and you are not having orgasms, try a little fantasy and friction at home by yourself. Learn what excites you, and that will help you achieve orgasm. Then, when you find a caring partner, you can guide that partner, and let him guide you, so you can both enjoy climaxing.

Q: How do you know whether a girl is faking an orgasm?
A: Outwardly, you don't always know, especially at first. You have to trust your partner and believe that she is enjoying herself as much as she seems to be. If you don't trust your partner, how can you achieve real sexual satisfaction? Any girl who is faking an orgasm is not acknowledging her right to feel sexual pleasure. If you both slow down and learn about each other's bodies and you communicate honestly and lovingly, it becomes much easier for an attentive partner to recognize (by feeling her contractions) when a girl is having an orgasm.

Q: Is it normal for teenage girls to not have orgasm during intercourse?
A: It's normal, especially in this society, where it has not been seen as necessary for a woman to have orgasms. Also, when young people first become sexual, there's a certain amount of inhibition. But it doesn't have to be habitual. Getting away from thinking you've *got* to have intercourse is the first step. Learning to pleasure each other by touching and caressing is the second step. By exploring safe and responsible ways to turn each other on, teens can have orgasms without risking the dangers of intercourse.

Chapter 4
What about Love?

L ove can be wonderful. It can energize you. It can uplift you. It can make you smile. But love can also be dangerous. It can make you feel as if you're invulnerable—as if nothing can happen to you. It can make you feel euphoric. It can make you forget about other responsibilities. "What, me clean up my room? Forget it! I'm in love!" Therefore, as with everything, love has to be looked at realistically—even while you're in love.

There are two sides to love. One is the "hot side." That comes from the gut. It's a chemistry you feel with certain people. It makes your heart skip a beat. It makes you float through the day on fantasies of touching and kissing that person. It renders you incapable of doing homework or taking out the garbage.

Dorothy Tennov, an author on the subject of love, describes this delicious and lovely side as "limerence." It's what you mean when you say you're "in love." Most everyone gets to experience limerence at least once in life. Actually, everyone is capable of falling "in love" at least 18 times.

The second side of love is the "cool part." It comes from your head. Though it's often hard to think clearly when you're in love, you still have to use your head to work out whether this is simply limerence or a love that can go the distance. Love is more than just feeling sexually attracted to someone. You can fall "in love," with anybody but you can't love everybody. As Carol Cassell, a writer and authority on sexuality, says "It's okay to lose your heart but not your head." If you lose your head, you can get into a relationship that might not be a healthy one for you or your partner.

So, how do you know if you're really in love? How do you know if this relationship is healthy and good for a longterm commitment? You look for the FACCTS.

FACCTS stands for *F*riendship, the *A*bility to *C*ommunicate and *C*ompromise, *T*rust, and *S*elf-esteem. Let's address them in order:

• Friendship: Try to determine whether or not you would be friends with this person if you weren't sexually attracted to him or her. Ask yourself these questions:

1. Is this a person who finds me interesting and who also interests me beyond the sexual attraction?

2. Are we curious about each other's everyday activities, the clothes we wear, the food we like, the books we read, our hobbies, our relationships with family members and friends?

• Ability to Communicate and Compromise: Being able to talk and listen to your love about your fears, joys, expectations is important for a long-term relationship. And the ability to compromise—to give and take, to accommodate different tastes and opinions—is necessary for a peaceful and happy relationship. Ask yourself these questions:

1. Do we talk about many different things, as well as feelings, with understanding and empathy?

2. Do we try to understand what the other is saying when the words aren't clear or exact?

3. Can we sometimes do things that are not of

interest to us because they are of interest to and will please our partner?

• **T**rust: A person you're going to get involved with has to be someone you feel safe and secure with, or you're going to drive yourself crazy worrying. Ask yourself these questions:

1. Do you believe that you will not cheat on each other or lie about things you have done?

2. If you are upset about something your partner has done, do you care enough to make the effort to work it out together before you run off to be comforted by someone else who is attractive?

3. Can you do some things on your own and respect your partner's freedom to do likewise without being suspicious or jealous?

• Self-esteem: This is probably the most important factor of all. If you don't think highly enough of yourself, no amount of love or limerence will help you. You can't rely on your partner to boost your self-esteem. Ask yourself these questions:

1. Will I allow myself to be pushed around or abused—physically or mentally—just so I won't lose my partner?

2. Will I push my partner around or abuse my partner—physically or mentally—to make myself feel better?

3. Does my partner value me for the special person I am?

4. Do I value my partner for his or her individuality?

You'll really have to do some clear thinking to get the FACCTS because limerence often clouds your brain and makes you say yes when the answer is really no.

Knowing the FACCTS takes time and effort, and sometimes one partner is interested and the other is not. The first reaction is to fight and try to get your partner to be interested. That's your gut reacting. Once you bring your brain into it, you realize that unresolved conflict is a clue that the relationship is not going to work.

The teen years are a time for exploring what you are looking for in a long-term partner. While you are getting to know who you are, you'll have a number of relationships in which you feel limerence. Some will last longer than others. Every one, though, will teach you something more about what you need in a relationship. Also, remember that no limerent relationship is worth committing suicide for. Limerence happens more than once in a lifetime. One 16-year-old boy asked me where I got the number "18" that I mentioned before.

"I made it up," I confessed.

He sighed with relief. "I've already been in love 24 times!" He meant that he was in limerence all those times.

While "in love" or limerence, it's important that you act safely and responsibly during your explorations. If you practice the CAR (*C*aring, *A*ttentiveness and *R*esponsibility) technique discussed in Chapter 3, you'll not only keep yourself happy, you'll be a great lover.

Love and limerence can be confusing. Here are some questions kids have asked me:

Q: What if your boyfriend keeps saying, "You would if you loved me"?
A: That really means just that he wants you to have intercourse with him. Sexuality doesn't equal intercourse. In fact, intercourse can be a health hazard. We want to be sexual because we are looking for pleasure. It would be better if we could concentrate on the pleasure without the health risk. Why not say to your boyfriend, "If you loved *me* you wouldn't be pressuring me to do something as risky as intercourse. Why don't we have some fun together by doing other pleasurable things that aren't so dangerous?" You and your boyfriend can reach orgasm without going all the way. Slow down. Find out what gives you both pleasure. Aim for orgasm, and keep a towel nearby to catch the semen. Exploration like this will make you both better lovers.

Q: If you date someone and your friends think he's dumb, what should you do?
A: Stop, look and listen! Do you enjoy talking to him about things that interest you? Does he express his ideas? Do you enjoy each other's company in many ways, and not just sexually? If you answered yes to all of these questions, then your

friends are wrong. They just don't know him yet. If you're not sure about the answers, it's possible that limerence is clouding your brain. That's okay, too, as long as you understand that the chemistry will fade and then maybe nothing will be left to keep the relationship going. While the limerence lasts, however, be careful about unwanted pregnancy and sexually transmitted diseases. Remember, this will not be the only relationship you'll have or want.

Q: What if you like a guy and he doesn't notice you?
A: That happens quite a lot. And it happens the other way around, too—you like a girl and she doesn't notice you. It takes time to find someone who shares love with you equally. In a case like this, you're feeling limerent all by yourself. Try to get to know the person better. Create opportunities to talk together. Go for walks. Do homework together. If you get no response, it doesn't mean there's anything wrong with you. It just means that the person has different tastes. Instead of expending all that energy to get his or her attention, look around for people who will be as attracted to you as you are to them.

Q: How can you tell whether a girl is a slut?
A: First of all, let's not use the word "slut." It's an insult to women who are sexually active. It's a leftover from our puritanical history, which gave

men sexual freedom and required women to be sexually pure. In those days, it was popular to believe that women had no interest in sex. But women *were* interested—they just weren't supposed to admit it.

While we haven't completely lost those old attitudes, we are improving. Women are beginning to recognize their sexual feelings. Still, if they acknowledge them or act upon them, they may get labeled as sluts. On the other hand, guys who are sexually active are often admired and called "studs."

Our society is now in transition between the old ways and the new. It is still more acceptable for males to be sexually active than females. When I ask young males why they have sex, they say "for fun" or "it feels good" or "for pleasure." Young females almost always say "for love." They are still worried that having sex for fun will get them a bad rep. As long as she does it safely and responsibly, a woman has the right to be just as sexually active as a man.

Q: How do you know you love someone enough to sleep with them?
A: When you first start going with someone and you experience that chemistry, it's a great feeling. But that's not all there is to love. To find out how strongly you feel about each other takes time. But while you are in limerence, you have many sexual feelings and urges. The question is how to ex-

press those feelings and still avoid the dangers of unwanted pregnancy or sexually transmitted diseases. The answer is to avoid intercourse. Sleeping with someone doesn't have to mean intercourse. It can mean "outercourse": pleasuring each other by doing other things like mutual masturbation. Once you have both achieved orgasm, you can really sleep—that is, go to sleep in each other's arms.

Q: Why do girls play hard to get?
A: In our culture, girls are at a great risk sexually. If they give in to their sexual desires quickly, they might be labeled "sluts," which can really damage their self-esteem. So they want to wait until they are sure they're in love, and that the guy is in love with them. The problem with this is that being "in love" doesn't always mean real love, and relationships that aren't based on real love will break up. When that happens, girls can feel very hurt. They believed that they were in love enough to have sex, and now they feel abandoned. Many times they rush into another relationship so they won't feel lonely and to restore their self-esteem. This can damage them further because rushing doesn't give them enough time to assess the new relationship for real love either.

Another risk for girls is unwanted pregnancy. Many times a guy simply won't use a condom, and the girl isn't secure enough to insist. No condom can result in something worse than pregnancy, too: AIDS and other STDs.

Girls don't have to play hard to get if they and their boyfriends engage in outercourse instead of intercourse.

Q: How can you say no and still have a boyfriend?
A: It depends on what you're saying no to. If you say no to intercourse and a guy dumps you, what have you lost? A boy who doesn't respect your feelings as much as he expects you to respect his is not good boyfriend material. He's not interested in you as a person. He only wants to use you as a receptacle for his sexual needs.

If you are saying no to outercourse, you, of course, have the right to abstain from all sexual interactions for either religious or philosophical reasons.

But if it isn't either of these, then you have to ask yourself if you're really sexually attracted to him. If not, he isn't your boyfriend—he's your friend who happens to be a boy.

When it comes to the boyfriend/girlfriend relationship, it's a good idea to wait until you find someone who is willing to get to know you as an individual and engage in outercourse with you. Later, if intercourse is included, you must both approach it cautiously and use a condom properly. (See Chapter 7 for the proper—and sexy—use of a condom).

Q: How can you convince girls to just have fun like we do?
A: If what you mean by "have fun" is intercourse without a sense of obligation, then you're lucky to find a girl who won't have fun that way. She is making you give more serious thought to what fun is. Intercourse is a dangerous activity. Unwanted pregnancy can cut down on fun pretty quickly. There are plenty of other ways to "have fun." Pleasuring each other and bringing each other to orgasm without intercourse is even more fun because it doesn't carry the often-life-threatening risks of intercourse.

Q: My boyfriend says he loves me, but when we're with other people, he keeps putting me down. Also, sometimes, when he drinks, he pushes me around. He apologizes, but then he does it again. What should I do? I love him.
A: Ask yourself what you love about him. When a guy abuses you, either psychologically or physically, and you take it, that's not love. You're letting limerence cloud your brain. Get the FACCTS. A person who abuses you isn't your *F*riend. A person who abuses you doesn't have much of an *A*bility to *C*ommunicate with you or *C*ompromise. A person who keeps on apologizing for the same behavior can't be very sorry or very *T*rustworthy.

Most importantly, people with *S*elf-esteem aren't abusers, nor do they take abuse from anyone. The interaction you are describing does not bode well for a good long-term relationship. Lose him.

Q: Is it true that you fall in love with the first one you have sex with just because they're your first?
A: It's often true. Having sex—usually intercourse—is frequently misinterpreted as love. The warmth of being held and caressed, being whispered to, is lovely and is one of the joys of life. But there's a difference between love and limerence, and we have to start recognizing it. Not knowing that difference can result in relationship breakdown, hurt, and sometimes violence. Instead of relying so heavily on our initial gut feelings, we have to take the time to get to know each other so we know how to work together to keep our relationships exciting and challenging. When we finally find someone we really want to make a long-term commitment to, we need to pledge exclusivity.

Q: Is having sex with someone once with no commitment OK?
A: Only if 3 criteria are met:
1. Both partners consent to it willingly and happily.
2. Both partners know and use all ways of preventing pregnancy and STDs.
3. Both partners achieve orgasm.

Otherwise it just becomes "scoring," and scoring is stealing from the one who doesn't benefit from all three criteria.

Q: What if one does more for the other? If he or she says they don't want anything in return, should the other person feel guilty? What are the dangers of doing this?
A: The dangers are that the one who "gets more" will continue to feel guilty and the one who does all the sacrificing will lose self-esteem. In both cases, resentment will eventually set in. That's where the CAR principle comes in. When people Care about their sexuality, they not only try to derive maximum pleasure for themselves, they make every effort to pleasure their partner, too. This means that both partners have to pay close Attention to their own pleasure needs as well as the needs of their partner. It requires that both partners learn to communicate—verbally and nonverbally—what they like and Respect the differences and individuality of their partner. This can take time but the reward is a long-term, comfortable, secure relationship.

Q: You talk about exploring a number of relationships. What about commitment?
A: We need to define commitment. While you are doing the inevitable exploring that is essential to learning what is meant by love, the commitment to each relationship means following the CAR principle: Caring, Attention, and Respect for each

other. You will be good lovers to each other, will not hurt each other and, while you are in the relationship (no matter how long it lasts), you will be loyal. Once you find the person you want to form an enduring long-term relationship with, your commitment is to give up further exploring. You work together to maintain the excitement and love you found when you first met.

Chapter 5
What about Masturbation?

asturbation is the act of bringing yourself to orgasm, usually using your hand. Sometimes it's called being "autosexual." That doesn't mean doing it in a car. There are lots of slang expressions for masturbation. They include "playing with yourself," "jerking off," and "beating your meat."

I have found that outwardly, at least in discussion groups, boys generally react negatively to masturbation. One young high-schooler said derisively, "You wanna make us all into perverts?" The lingering machismo of males discourages them from admitting its common practice or its legitimacy.

Masturbation is probably the most misunderstood pleasuring activity. The myths and taboos connected with it go back a long way—all the way, in fact, to the days when the sole purpose of sex was to make babies and promote the survival of the species. Over the centuries, masturbation has gained a bad rep. I'd like to change the expression to "self-love" or, better yet, "fantasy and friction." Both are much more healthy and less guilt-inducing.

Some of the myths that have grown up around masturbation include:

- You'll go blind if you do it.
- Hair will grow on your palms if you do it.
- You'll go crazy if you do it.

Scientific research points out that there is absolutely no harm in masturbating. In fact, masturbation can be good for you. It's a top-notch way to learn about your body. It's an excellent outlet for tension and anxiety. It's a wonderful way to discover what kind of touching and caressing turn you on. There are even some physicians who recommend it to women suffering from severe menstrual cramps. Orgasm makes the uterus contract, and that relieves the engorged uterine tissue which may be cramping.

Don't feel guilty about masturbation. Pretty much everyone does it, whether or not they admit it. People masturbate even within marriage. Masturbation can represent a substitute for sexual interaction with a partner or an alternative approach to pleasuring. And Masters and Johnson, the famous sex researchers, found out that the sensual pleasure derived from masturbation can be more intense than any other approach.

Despite our scientific knowledge about the advantages of masturbation, there are a number of people who don't believe in it for religious reasons. It's certainly their choice not to engage in it, and we must respect different values. Therefore, I say, "Masturbation is normal whether you do it or not."

Mutual masturbation—bringing both partners to orgasm using hands, lips, tongue, a vibrator, and so on—is also a wonderful pleasuring technique.

Although many people still consider masturbation dirty and sinful, it is nothing to feel guilty about. And, given the dangers of intercourse these days, it is an alternative that really deserves to be considered.

Kids everywhere are curious about masturbation. Here are some of the questions they've asked me:

Q: Do most people masturbate?
A: Yes, but they hardly ever talk about it because masturbation still carries a bad connotation and a lot of guilt. That's too bad. All the latest scientific research points to the fact that masturbation is good for tension and anxiety release.

Q: Is masturbation a sin?
A: Some religious people think it is. The reason it's promoted as sinful comes from religious teachings thousands of years old. In those days, the taboo against masturbation made some sense. Life was filled with danger, and the survival of the human species was by no means guaranteed. "Spilling one's seed" through masturbation wasted the life force that was necessary to keep us alive on this planet. Also, in ancient times, it was believed that each sperm cell carried within it a fully formed human being call a homunculus. The uterus was thought to be merely a place for its development. Therefore, the spilling of seed was tantamount to losing lots of little people.

Another biblical reference to masturbation and its sinfulness is found in the story of Onan. Onan was ordered by his father to impregnate his dead brother's wife. That was the rule in those days. But he refused. Instead, he spilled his seed upon the ground. He broke a religious law and that was sinful. Some biblical scholars say that Onan's main sin was in disobeying his father. In those days, that was one of the most serious sins, and that's why God struck him down. Even today, deliberate masturbation is sometimes referred to as "onanism" because it is a spilling of seed for reasons other than reproduction. These references make people who masturbate feel guilty and want to do it secretly.

The focus on procreation no longer pertains. We don't have to worry about our numbers. There are 5 billion of us. These days, masturbation is recognized as a perfectly normal and healthy sexual outlet for everyone.

Q: How do you masturbate alone?
A: Everyone masturbates differently. The main stimuli are your hands. You touch yourself on the penis, clitoris, breasts—whatever is sensitive—until you achieve orgasm. The best way to masturbate is slowly, paying close attention to what really turns you on. You can even use music and soft lights for atmosphere. This will help you to masturbate more deliberately and excitingly in the future, and help you show your lover, when you find one, how to make love to you in the most satisfying way possible. The more you know about your own pleasuring needs, the more you can teach your partner about how to satisfy you.

Q: How do you do mutual masturbation?
A: Mutual masturbation is the act of bringing

your partner to orgasm using your hands and other means you both like while your partner caresses you to climax. Unfortunately, mutual masturbation brings about a damning reaction from many people. They consider it dirty and naughty to touch each other in those intimate places. Our society's long-held belief that sex is for procreation only negates pleasuring as a legitimate reason for being sexual. We are actually a very antipleasure society, especially in relation to sexuality. Yet mutual masturbation is probably the cleanest and safest way to have sex these days.

You and your partner need to explore each other's bodies paying close attention to what turns the other on. Slow and deliberate movements are recommended. Verbal and nonverbal cues—moving your body, moving your partner's hand or head—can help you give each other maximum pleasure.

Sex therapists recommend mutual masturbation to people who want to become better lovers. Scientific studies show that orgasms achieved through solo and mutual masturbation are more intense than those achieved through intercourse. The intimacy you can find with a partner and the removal of focus from intercourse really open you up sensually. And don't forget that if you have masturbated alone, you'll know in advance what feels best.

Q: How much masturbation is normal?

A: How much of anything is normal? Once before each meal? Twice before bedtime? If it doesn't interfere with the rest of your life, like going to school, doing your homework, helping out around the house or participating in extracurricular sports, it's normal.

This doesn't mean you *have* to masturbate or *should* masturbate. Not everyone wants to. Not every family considers masturbation OK. Some families do, however, and accept it as a natural part of life as long as it's done in private.

Here's something interesting: Most girls don't have orgasms when they first start having sex. A recent study found, however, that those who do, got a reassuring message about sexuality from their mothers, and part of this message was that masturbation is a good way to find out what pleasures you.

Q: Is there something wrong with me if I don't want to masturbate?

A: No. One girl told me she never masturbates. Lots of kids who grew up in homes where it was banned for religious reasons don't masturbate. Lots of people who were taught that masturbation is disgusting, don't do it. The important thing is not to do it, if you don't want to, but to accept the scientific evidence that masturbation is normal and that people can do it without being harmed.

Q: Is masturbation harmful?
A: No. It isn't. Long ago it was called self-abuse. People were told that touching yourself would cause insanity, hairy palms, and worse. Here's a joke that really sums up the old attitude:

A father walked in on his son who was masturbating: "Don't ever do that or you'll go blind."

"Okay," replied his son who was very frightened.

Soon, however, the threat faded, his normal sexual urges returned and he started masturbating again. Once again his father caught him in the act. "Didn't I tell you not to do that because you'll go blind?" yelled the father.

"I thought I'd just do it until I needed glasses," said the boy.

This proves, that even under threat, people want to masturbate.

Scientific evidence shows that masturbation is definitely not harmful in any way. In fact, it's the opposite. It relieves sexual tension, and is one of the safest ways of pleasuring. It's a great way to learn about your body and its sensual potential.

Q: Don't some kids get punished for masturbating?
A: Yes. And, years ago, kids were often severely punished. Girls were punished more strictly than boys because girls weren't supposed to be interested in sex at all. Today some kids are probably still punished for masturbating. We do know,

though, that masturbation is not a bad thing regardless of whether kids are punished for it or not.

Q: How old should you be before you masturbate?
A: There is no specific age. Young children discover their pleasure zones early in life and, unless it is forbidden by a worried adult, they masturbate. This self-love continues throughout their lives, even when people get old. In fact, when people are older, masturbation is the perfect sexual activity: both alone and with a partner. Learning to masturbate and mutually masturbate means that you can give pleasure and receive it until you die, without necessarily including intercourse. This is important for older people to know because, as the body slows up with aging, erections are not as frequent or reliable, and orgasms through intercourse are more difficult to achieve for both partners.

Q: Does masturbation make you feel different than intercourse?
A: Yes. Masters and Johnson discovered that the pleasure gotten from masturbation can be even more intense than other kinds of sexual pleasuring. This is not surprising. You know better than any partner can what feels good. Of course, there's a great deal of pleasure to be derived from interaction with a partner—it's just a different kind.

Q: Can anyone tell whether you have been masturbating?
A: No. There's no outward sign that will let other people know that you've been engaging in self-love.

Q: Will masturbating make my penis larger?
A: No. You are born with the genetic blueprint for a certain size penis, and that's the size you'll have when you are an adult. No amount of pulling and massaging will make your penis bigger. Besides, penis size has nothing to do with the ability to pleasure yourself or a partner.

Q: Will masturbation make my vagina bigger?
A: No. The main thing that affects the size of your vagina is childbirth. But no matter what size your vagina is, it won't affect your sexual pleasure. The vagina is not where the nerve endings are. Those are located in the clitoris and at the entrance to the vagina (called the introitus).

Q: Is it only considered masturbation if you have an orgasm?
A: No. Any manipulation of the genitals that brings pleasure—orgasmic or not—is considered masturbation.

Q: What does a vibrator do?
A: A vibrator is an electrical device sometimes shaped like a penis and sometimes like a round

wheel. It stimulates your pleasure centers and makes you feel good. You can use a vibrator on any part of your body. One popular place is the clitoris, and another is the entrance to the vagina. If you insert a vibrator into your vagina, it's often a good idea to use a little lubricating cream. Vibrators can be purchased in department stores and drugstores.

Q: If you masturbate, can you urinate in the middle?
A: If you're a girl, yes. If you're a boy, usually not. In boys, the bladder closes off during an erection.

Q: Do guys masturbate as much if they have a very active sex life?
A: Yes. Guys often masturbate even if they have lots of sexual partners. Masturbation involves different stimuli, different fantasies, and different pleasures. What's more, lots of guys have mighty sex drives, and masturbation helps satisfy them.

Q: Is it natural for homosexuals to masturbate?
A: Yes. It's natural for anyone to masturbate.

Q: Will playing with yourself cause problems in intercourse?
A: No. In fact, it can help. Masturbation teaches you what gives you the greatest pleasure. Knowing that makes it easier for you to guide your partner in actions that really excite you without

intercourse. One study showed that girls who had a lot of experience with masturbation—self-love and mutual masturbation—were more likely to get pleasure from intercourse the first time than those who had no experience.

Q: Do all boys play around with their buddies sometimes?
A: It's perfectly normal for boys to play around with their buddies. This kind of behavior happens all over. Some guys do "circle jerks." They all sit in a circle and masturbate together. Sometimes they even have a competition to see whose semen squirts the farthest. Sometimes boys jerk each other off. If you experiment with other guys, it doesn't mean you're homosexual. It just means you're exploring your sexuality.

Q: Do girls play around with each other?
A: Although they don't talk about it much, girls do masturbate in front of each other or touch and rub each other. It doesn't mean they're lesbians. Just about everyone experiments sexually. Girls are just more ashamed of it than boys because girls still grow up thinking it isn't quite right for them to feel sexual.

Q: What do you do if you go out with a guy and he starts masturbating while you're kissing?
A: You can help him—but only if you want to. Or

you can just let *him* do it—if you want to. You can also ask him to stop—if you want to.

Q: My friend told me about the "G spot." What does it have to do with masturbation?
A: The G spot is a small area inside the vagina, on the upper wall which, when rubbed, produces great orgasms. It was named for a Dr. Grafenberg who first discovered it. Researchers estimate that about 40 percent of all women have it. If you or your partner can locate it through mutual sexual exploration, you can rub it or stroke it until orgasm is achieved. If you want to know more about it, check out a book called *ESO: How You and Your Lover Can Give Each Other Hours of Extended Sexual Orgasm* by A. Brauer and D. Brauer (Warner Books, 1983). ESO stands for Extended Sexual Orgasm.

Since not every woman has a G spot, you and your partner may not find one. That doesn't matter. One boy told me, "My girlfriend and I bought the book, and we tried and tried to find the G spot, and couldn't."

"Did you have fun looking for it?" I asked.

"Yeah," he said, grinning, "we sure did!"

That's all that counts. Looking for the G spot can be sexy and stimulating in itself, and all orgasms, no matter where they come from, are pleasurable. In solo masturbation, if you should ever use a vibrator for insertion, you might find the G spot on the upper vaginal wall, if you pay attention. But remember; it really doesn't matter if you don't happen to have one.

Q: Will it hurt your athletic performance if you jack off?
A: No. The myth that sex will ruin your athletic performance is just that: a myth. It was once believed that ejaculation saps your strength because semen was considered the "fountain of life." The body keeps manufacturing more and replaces what's ejaculated. You recover quickly from sex.

Q: When and where can you masturbate safely?
A: Masturbate in private. Find a place where you won't be disturbed. Do it when you have time to explore your body and learn what you like and where you like to be touched. The point of masturbation—besides being good for the relief of sexual tension—is to find out what pleasures you on so you can help your partner give you maximum pleasure someday. Music can help set the mood.

Q: How come I've heard that some weirdos masturbate?
A: Weirdos, in my opinion, are people who masturbate in public, where it can offend others. That's inappropriate behavior. People who masturbate in private for their own pleasure are not weirdos. They are normal people engaging in a natural sexual outlet. Pretty much anything you

do by yourself that doesn't harm yourself or others is okay.

Q: Is it bad to masturbate your same-sex friend?
A: No. And it doesn't necessarily mean you're gay, either. If you're both doing it to explore, without feeling guilty, it's a part of learning about sexuality and part of growing up. But there has to be mutual consent. If one person pressures the other to do it, that can result in a lost friendship. Sexual exploration must always be mutual.

Q: I looked in my mother's drawer for a pair of socks and found a vibrator. Is it natural for a mother to do this? Will I end up like her?
A: The teenager who wrote this question to me signed it "Totally Upset." She thought her mother was strange. She's not. Using a vibrator is normal—even for mothers. It's a way of pleasuring yourself.

Q: What if someone walks in on you while you're masturbating?
A: If it's an adult—one of your parents, for example—it would be great if he or she would just walk out. If not, you can ask them politely to leave. If that person says something mean about masturbation, respond by saying, "This is normal. I'm just exploring my sexuality!"

Most important, even though this situation can

be very embarrassing, you must not feel guilty. There's nothing wrong with masturbation.

Q: Is it okay to get aroused by looking at naked people in magazines or videos?
A: Yes. Arousal is normal. How you act out that arousal is the issue. If you go to a private place and masturbate, or, if you have a partner and the two of you pleasure each other, that's a healthy outlet. It's not okay to take your arousal and force someone to have sex with you.

Chapter 6

What about AIDS and Other Sexually-transmitted Diseases?

Throughout this book, I have emphasized the dangers of intercourse. AIDS and other sexually transmitted diseases are at the top of the risk list.

Sexually transmitted diseases—or STDs—are illnesses that are mainly passed on through intercourse. Among the STDs you risk catching through unprotected intercourse are gonorrhea, syphilis, venereal warts, chlamydia (*kluh-MID-ee-uh*), herpes, trichomonas (*trick-uh-MOAN-iss*), and AIDS. All of them are health risks, but most can be cured if caught early enough. Not AIDS. AIDS is deadly.

AIDS stands for Acquired Immune Deficiency Syndrome. It is caused by the human immunodeficiency virus (HIV). AIDS is passed from an infected person to a noninfected person through the exchange of bodily fluids such as semen and blood.

Having the AIDS virus is not what kills a person. This virus is more dangerous than other viruses because it attacks the body's immune system and leaves it vulnerable to all kinds of opportunistic infections such as rare forms of pneumonia and cancer. These are the illnesses that eventually cause death. Ordinarily, when a person's immune system is intact, it resists catching these rare diseases even though the organisms are around everywhere. Sometimes the AIDS virus lies dormant for as long as 10 to 15 years without causing illness. But once you have HIV in your system, it's probably only a matter of time before you become sick.

AIDS is not just a disease of homosexuals. Anyone can get it. Look at Magic Johnson and Arthur Ashe. Look at Ryan White. Look at most other places in the world where it is mainly a heterosexual disease. You must not think that just because you're *not* gay, you're protected.

Fortunately, the AIDS virus is hard to catch. You can't get it by sharing an infected person's toothbrush or fork or knife. You can't get it by kissing infected people or wiping away their tears. You can't get by it using the same bathroom or telephone as an infected person. Two conditions must be met simultaneously for its transmission:

1. a *large enough* dose of the virus
2. a blood connection

Knowing this, we can examine the various levels of risk involved in different types of sexual contact.

• French kissing—Though saliva is exchanged during this activity, the chances of transmission are small. Saliva is not one of the body fluids that carries huge doses of the virus.

• Mutual masturbation—Low risk because there is virtually no exchange of bodily fluids.

• Oral sex—If one of the partners is HIV positive and the other has cuts or abrasions in his or her mouth, the chance of transmission is there. Semen carries a lot of the virus. If an HIV-positive male ejaculates into another person's mouth, and that person has abrasions on the gums or anywhere else, the virus can get into the bloodstream. If a female is HIV-positive, her vaginal secretions will contain the virus. If she lubricates a lot, there may be enough fluid to infect a partner who has mouth abrasions. If the woman has her period, HIV can be passed through the menstrual blood into mouth abrasions.

• Intercourse—Unprotected intercourse is a high-risk activity when it comes to AIDS and all other sexually transmitted diseases. Semen carries a large dose of HIV. If a girl has any abrasions or cuts, or even a mild infection in her vaginal wall or cervix, the chance of AIDS infection is high. Girls might not even know whether they have vaginal cuts or infections since there are not many nerve endings inside the vagina. Males can also pick up the AIDS virus from the female's lubrication if she is HIV-positive. If the guy has any abrasions on his penis or has an irritated urethra, he is vulnerable.

• Anal sex—Perhaps the highest risk activity of all, anal sex is not restricted to gay men. Many heterosexual couples also engage in this activity. In fact, recent reports show that about 30 percent of sexually active teenagers use anal sex as a means of avoiding pregnancy. The tissue of the anus is full of blood vessels and is quite thin. Therefore, it can be ripped easily if something large—like a penis—is introduced, especially if done forcibly. Once the tissue is torn, semen can enter the bloodstream. If the semen is HIV-positive, transmission can occur.

Happily, condoms for the penis and dental dams (thin latex sheets invented by dentists) for female genitals, provide good protection from the transmission of most STDs, AIDS included. But only if they are used properly.

Of course the surest way *not* to get AIDS or other sexually transmitted diseases, is to refrain from intercourse. Try other pleasuring techniques instead. If you *must* have intercourse, practice the proper way to use condoms and dental dams, and be responsible.

And don't forget: Other than through sex, the surest way to get AIDS is to use someone else's needle to inject drugs directly into your arm or leg. If the previous needle user was HIV-positive, the virus will enter your blood right along with the drugs.

Here are some questions teens have asked me about AIDS:

Q: What does AIDS stand for?
A: Acquired Immune Deficiency Syndrome. It means that the AIDS virus attacks the body's immune system, makes it unable to fight diseases, and leaves it open to opportunistic diseases.

Q: What is an opportunistic disease?
A: It's a fairly rare disease that, ordinarily, people can fight off, but which will attack the body when the immune system is weak. People with HIV develop weaker and weaker immune systems

over a period of about 10 to 15 years, so a lot of diseases have the opportunity to move in. Some opportunistic diseases associated with AIDS include pneumocystic pneumonia, tuberculosis, Kaposi's sarcoma (a type of cancer), and very severe cases of shingles.

Q: Where did AIDS originate?
A: There's an element of mystery about this. Researchers believe that AIDS came from Africa, where a lot of tropical diseases flourish. Some researchers believe it was originally a virus that infected only a species of monkey, that got transferred to a human being when blood mingled during butchering. It may also be that some virus that was originally not dangerous mutated into its present deadly form.

Q: How do you get AIDS?
A: Through high-risk sexual behavior. High risk includes anal sex, oral sex, and intercourse. These sexual behaviors put the partners at risk by exposing them to bodily fluids that carry HIV. When an HIV-positive male, for example, ejaculates into an unprotected vagina, if there are any lesions or cuts in the vagina or on the cervix, the woman can catch the AIDS virus. If an unprotected penis is inserted into the anus, it can tear the anal tissue and, when ejaculation occurs, the virus can be passed from the semen right into the bloodstream. When an unprotected penis ejaculates

into a mouth, HIV can enter the bloodstream through any cuts or abrasions that may be there.

When a female is HIV-positive, a male can catch it from her if he has any cuts or abrasions on his penis. It is somewhat more difficult for a male to get AIDS from a female because she may not produce enough vaginal secretions to have a large dose of the virus. However, the risk is there, and some people are probably vulnerable even in lower-risk situations. What's more, when you have many sexual partners, you put yourself at a higher risk. Take Magic Johnson, for example. He had sex frequently with many, many women. It's possible that he irritated his urethra (the opening at the end of the penis), and that the irritation allowed the virus to enter his bloodstream. In addition, when a mouth comes in contact with the genitalia of an HIV-positive woman, the virus can pass from the vaginal lubrication into the bloodstream via any cuts and abrasions in the mouth.

There are four major ways of transmitting AIDS:

1. Through vaginal, oral, or anal intercourse.
2. By using someone else's needle to inject intravenous drugs into your own bloodstream. An HIV-positive drug user can leave enough blood and virus in a needle to pass AIDS on to the next user.
3. Through blood transfusions. Before the blood supply was screened, many people con-

tracted AIDS when they received HIV-positive blood during transfusions. This occurs
far less often now that we can test for the
virus, but it still happens.

4. Through childbirth. A mother can transmit HIV to her newborn as it passes through
the birth canal. AIDS can also be transmitted
from mother to child through breast milk.

The best way to avoid the transmission of AIDS
and other STDs is to use a condom properly when
you have anal sex, oral sex, or vaginal intercourse
—or, better yet, to practice outercourse. And
don't inject drugs!

Q: What is the chance of getting AIDS?
A: It depends on what kind of sexual risks you
take. You can reduce your chances of getting
AIDS by engaging in safer sex—that is, masturbation and mutual masturbation (outercourse). Using condoms for intercourse and anal sex, and
condoms and dental dams for oral sex, are safer
sex practices, too.

Naturally, the more people you have sex with,
the greater your chance of getting AIDS and other
STDs. Remember: when you sleep with someone,
you're also sleeping with everyone *that* person
has slept with.

Q: What is safe sex?
A: Since there are many activities putting you at

risk for contracting the AIDS virus, and since everyone has a different level of susceptibility, we prefer to use the term *safer* sex rather than *safe* sex. Nothing is 100 percent foolproof. So, safe sex is sexual contact that reduces your risk of catching the AIDS virus or any other STD. There are different kinds of safer sex: intercourse and anal sex with a condom, and oral sex with a condom or dental dam. Condoms are highly effective against the spread of AIDS and other STDs, but only if used properly. Of course, even when someone uses condoms absolutely correctly, and also uses them every time they make love, there can always be an accident.

Unfortunately, many kids don't know how to use condoms properly because no one has ever taught them. Consequently, they may not work. One 16-year-old girl told me that she and her boyfriend gave up using condoms because they just didn't work. They kept on breaking. I was puzzled. I know we have very-good-quality condoms in this country. In talking to her further, I discovered that neither she nor her boyfriend understood that you have to squeeze a 1/2" space at the end, when the condom is placed on the erect penis. This will remove any air bubbles and leave room for the semen. Without this space, the condom is sure to break. Also, the guy has to hold on to the rim of the condom when pulling out so that his semen doesn't spill into the vagina. When using a lubricant, get only water-based ones like K-Y Jelly. Do not use oil-based lubricants like Vaseline, mineral and vegetable oils, or cold cream. These can easily break the condom.

Outercourse is the best kind of safe sex. By outercourse I mean mutual caressing, kissing, touching, and playing until you and your partner reach orgasm. Outercourse is probably the safest because not only are you less likely to catch an STD, you're also unlikely to end up with a pregnancy on your hands.

Q: Do you think everyone will eventually get AIDS?

A: NO! AIDS is relatively hard to get and relatively easy to avoid getting if you know what the risks are. If you practice safer sex and avoid IV drugs, you can protect yourself from AIDS. When people learn these facts, the spread of AIDS will decline.

Q: If AIDS is a blood-borne disease, why are sexual intercourse and oral and anal sex as dangerous as intravenous drug use?

A: People can get the AIDS virus in these ways because there can be an exchange of bodily fluids and a direct blood connection. When you have unprotected intercourse, anal sex, or oral sex, HIV can be transmitted in semen and vaginal lubricant through any vaginal, cervical, or mouth scratches and cuts you might have or get. Intravenous drug users who share needles can also introduce HIV directly into their bloodstreams.

Q: Why can't people be more understanding about AIDS?
A: Basically it's because of our puritanical attitude about sexuality in general and homosexuality in particular. Because AIDS ran rampant through the gay community first, a lot of people think it's only a gay disease. And a lot of people are antigay. AIDS is not just a gay disease. It's a disease that can affect anybody: old, young, gay, straight, black, white, Asian. In places like Africa, AIDS is mainly transmitted heterosexually. If people stopped judging homosexuals and stopped being so uptight about sexuality, AIDS wouldn't be such an outcast disease. And that's what we're trying to teach.

Q: Why didn't people start to use condoms before the AIDS virus started? Were there any made?
A: Condoms have been around for hundreds of years. People didn't wear them because they didn't think there was a need. Many women took the pill, and that took care of the pregnancy risk. If males had made condom use a regular practice, fewer people today would have AIDS.

Also, many people (both males and females) think that a condom reduces the sensitivity of the penis and thus the pleasure. This, however, is largely a myth. If used properly, there's plenty of pleasure in condoms. One suggestion, which seems to work well, is to put a drop of water-based lubricant inside the tip of the condom, before putting it on. Its creaminess increases sensitivity. You can also use prelubricated condoms.

In fact, putting a condom on can be a pretty sexy act in itself. Just think of how exciting it could be to unroll the condom on the erect penis and caress the wrinkles out of it. When I ask teenage boys whether they'd like their girlfriends to put a condom on for them, they all say "Yeah!"

However, many girls, when I ask if they'd like to put a condom on for their boyfriend, say, "Well, er, I don't know if I want to touch that thing." And, clearly, they don't necessarily mean the condom. No one teaching sex education has included the remarkable mechanisms that leads to erection in males or lubrication in females. These mechanisms are wonderful to learn about —they put you in awe of the wonderful way your body works. Go to the library and look it up.

Q: If the male wears a condom, is there any risk at all of either partner getting the AIDS virus?
A: Safe sex is safe sex, not foolproof sex. There's always a risk. The condom might have a hole in it. It might break. It might slip off and spill the semen into the vagina. But condoms are the best thing we have right now, *if* you insist on engaging in any type of intercourse.

Q: Can a person contract AIDS from having just anal sex?

A: Absolutely! In fact, anal sex is the highest-risk sexual activity you can engage in. The anus is lined with very thin tissue, which has lots and lots of blood vessels that are close to the surface. Introducing a penis into the anus always introduces the risk of a tear in the tissue. If no condom is used, any virus in the semen that is ejaculated could move right into the bloodstream.

Q: Can two men in a sexual act create the AIDS virus? If yes, how?

A: No man or woman can *create* the AIDS virus. If either of the two men in a sexual act already happens to have the virus, then he can pass it on through unprotected anal and oral sex.

Q: Can you get AIDS by kissing or french kissing?

A: There are no reported cases of transmission from this activity. HIV is a hard virus to catch. There needs to be a big dose of it present, plus a way to get into the bloodstream, in order to be infected. In an infected person, each of the bodily fluids carries a different amount of HIV. Saliva has a small dose. Kissing is a relatively low-risk activity.

Q: Can a girl with AIDS have sex with a boy with AIDS without any side effect?

A: If two people are already HIV-positive with the

same strain of the virus and are having inter-course, they can obviously no longer give each other that particular virus. However, it seems as if there are different strains of HIV, and if these others are also carried by either partner, they can exchange them sexually and perhaps get even sicker.

Q: Can a girl get sick or die if she gives a boy a blowjob if he has AIDS?
A: Yes. The AIDS virus can be passed through oral sex. If a girl gives an HIV-positive boy a blowjob and he ejaculates in her mouth, the virus can enter the girl's bloodstream through any small cut or abrasion she might have in her mouth. A condom, used correctly, can cut down on the AIDS risk.

Q: Can you get AIDS by letting a girl give you a blowjob?
A: It's unlikely you'll get the AIDS virus if a girl gives you a blowjob. Saliva has a low dose of HIV. There's a small risk, however, if you've got any cuts or irritations anywhere on your penis, and the girl is HIV-positive. Mostly, it's the girl who takes risk in the case of blowjobs.

Q: Can you get AIDS by heavy petting?
A: No. Heavy petting is a safe-sex activity as long as bodily fluids have no possibility of entering the bloodstream.

Q: Can you get AIDS from someone's perspiration?
A: Not likely. Sweat doesn't carry a large dose of HIV.

Q: If you were walking down the road and you found a condom and used it, could you get AIDS?
A: If it was a used condom, used by an HIV-positive guy and you put it on while it was still wet and you had a cut or irritation anywhere on your penis, you might get the AIDS virus. It's better all around never to use a used condom. Even if the condom was in a wrapper, you would not know how old it was. And old condoms can break easily.

Q: Can you get AIDS if you're using a condom that has a hole in it?
A: Yes. If infected semen can get out and enter the bloodstream, the AIDS virus can go with it.

Q: How did Liberace get AIDS?
A: Liberace was a homosexual, and he got AIDS by having unprotected sex with another man who was HIV-positive. It's important to realize that presently the largest reduction in AIDS incidence is within the gay and bisexual population.

Q: Can you get AIDS from animals?
A: It's unlikely. Generally speaking, animal diseases differ from human diseases.

Q: If a man gets "fixed" (has a vasectomy), can he still get AIDS by having intercourse?
A: Yes. AIDS has nothing to do with whether or not you can make babies. When a man gets "fixed", it means that there is no longer a way for sperm from his testicles to get into his semen. A fixed man can transmit the virus through his semen even though he won't get a woman pregnant. Semen will carry HIV even if it is sperm-free. And, if a fixed man has sex with an infected woman, he can get the AIDS virus from her.

Q: Is there any one place in the United States that AIDS is particularly concentrated?
A: So far it is concentrated mostly in large cities. There's more drug use and prostitution in such places, and both are high-risk activities.

Q: Where can you go to see if you have AIDS?
A: There are many places these days that will test you for AIDS: hospitals, your doctor, Planned Parenthood and AIDS clinics. If you give blood, you will be tested to find out if you're HIV-positive. Look in the yellow pages for clinics that do the tests.

Q: What do they do with people who have AIDS until they die?
A: Some patients with full-blown AIDS stay in the hospital until they die. Some go home or to hospices to die, and some, with the many new

treatments now available, are able to live fairly active lives until death.

Q: Are all the other sexually transmitted diseases deadly like AIDS?

A: No. Some can be pretty dangerous, though. These days, however, many of the other STDs can be cleared up with antibiotics if they are caught early enough. But antibiotics kill bacteria, not viruses. So STDs that are caused by viruses (like herpes or venereal warts) are not deadly, but may cause prolonged illnesses and even sterility.

Q: Can you get AIDS from an open cut if an infected person's saliva gets on it?

A: Probably not. There's some risk, but it appears to be very low. The virus occurs in low doses in the saliva.

Q: If someone with AIDS cuts himself on something, and you cut yourself with the same thing, can you get AIDS?

A: Yes, although a lot depends on how much of the virus is on the sharp object that caused the cut. Anytime there's a blood connection, there's always the risk of transmitting AIDS. That's why it's not a good idea to share razors or inject drugs.

Q: How many people can one person infect with AIDS?

A: It depends on how many people that infected person has unprotected sex with. Every person who has unprotected sex with an AIDS carrier runs the risk of getting AIDS, too. Wilt Chamberlain has said that he's had sex with 20,000 women. If he had AIDS, he could have given it to all of them. Magic Johnson got AIDS through unprotected sex. He put every woman he had sex with after he became infected at risk, too.

Q: Does birth control help prevent AIDS?
A: It depends. Neither the pill, the IUD, or a diaphragm will protect the vagina from coming in contact with infected semen. Nor will they protect a male if the woman is HIV-positive. A contraceptive sponge or suppository might offer some protection because they are impregnated with spermicides (which seem to also kill viruses), but there might not be enough medication to kill all the viruses. A condom, used properly, does help prevent AIDS by keeping the infected semen away from the vagina and cervix and by keeping the penis from making contact with the vaginal lubricants.

Q: Do you get AIDS if someone spits on you?
A: Highly unlikely. First of all, saliva doesn't carry a high concentration of HIV. Secondly, the AIDS virus is weak and can't survive in the air for long.

Q: Can you get AIDS from insects?
A: No. Not even from mosquitoes who have just bitten an infected person. Not enough of the virus is present to infect someone else.

Q: If people have AIDS, how long do they have to live?
A: First we have to distinguish between being a carrier and having full-blown AIDS. A carrier is HIV-positive but is not sick yet. That's why many HIV-positive people don't know that they are HIV-positive until they're tested. Someone with full-blown AIDS has one or more of the opportunistic infections associated with AIDS.

The usual time it takes for someone to go from being a carrier to having full-blown AIDS seems to be anywhere from 10 to 15 years. It may be that not every HIV-positive person will get full-blown AIDS. Data are still being collected on this disease. After people come down with full-blown AIDS, the time they have to live is very variable and depends on what medication is being taken, what kind of care is gotten, and how well they take care of themselves. Some of the new drugs—like AZT and related medications—seem to prolong life. Sadly, however, at this point, death is inevitable because no way has been found yet to restore the ruined immune system.

Q: If you wear two rubbers, are your chances of getting AIDS less?

A: Yes. But it's not necessary. One condom with no rip or tear is just as effective against AIDS, much easier to put on, and lets the man feel a lot more pleasure.

Q: If everybody knows the risk of AIDS, then why does everybody still use drugs and still have sex?
A: Not everybody knows the risk of AIDS. In this country, not enough is being done to educate people about all the activities that put a person at risk for AIDS. People are still reluctant to speak of all the sexual behaviors that are being engaged in because many of them are considered "dirty." If we had realistic sex education in schools, more people would know about AIDS and about how to prevent it. What's more, many young people who are sexually active don't think that AIDS can happen to them. They feel they are invincible! This belief is false. Good education gives kids the truth.

Q: Can someone get AIDS if the two partners are not infected?
A: Not if they have sex only with each other. If one goes out and has sex with someone else with the AIDS virus, then that person can contract it and can then give it to his or her partner.

Q: Are there any more known ways that you can catch the AIDS virus other than blood transfu-

sion, sexual intercourse, sharing dirty needles, or being a fag?

A: Being a homosexual is not a way to contract AIDS. No matter what your sexual orientation, engaging in unprotected anal, vaginal, or oral intercourse, and using IV drugs are ways to get the AIDS virus.

Q: How many different types of AIDS are there?

A: There seem to be two or more types of HIV that cause AIDS, but studies keep coming up with new data every day. For example, it might be that there has to be another organism, called a mycoplasma, present along with the AIDS virus, to put someone in the highest risk category. We need to get the results of a number of studies currently going on before we know for sure.

Q: Do you believe that married couples should be tested for AIDS before marriage?

A: Yes. It is especially important if either one has had other partners in the past or has had a blood transfusion. If one of the partners is HIV-positive and the other is negative, then, if they marry, they will have to engage in safer sex—like mutual masturbation, intercourse, and anal sex with condoms and oral sex with a condom and dental dam —throughout the course of their married life. If both partners test negative, they don't have to worry, as long as they remain monogamous. If both test positive, there is nothing further they can do, but they must not go outside their relationship and put other people at risk.

If people decide not to be tested when they marry, they should definitely be tested when they decide to have children. Mothers can transmit AIDS to their newborns while the infant passes through the birth canal and through breastfeeding.

Q: Do you think there will ever be a cure for AIDS?
A: It's possible, but it's hard to say. Like flu viruses, the AIDS virus mutates. That is, it changes rapidly to adapt to new environments. This makes it difficult for scientists to come up with a vaccine or other cure. Once scientists have created a formula that acts on one strain of HIV, it may change and becomes immune to the drug, just as new strains of flu appear every year and require new flu vaccines. We need to be hopeful, but instead of thinking about cures, it's better at this time to think about prevention in order to stay AIDS-free.

Chapter 7
What about Contraception?

If you don't want to become pregnant, there is only one method that is 100 percent effective: not to have vaginal intercourse. But, if you are still not listening to my message and you decide to have intercourse, using birth control will greatly reduce your chances of pregnancy. As many as 85 percent of sexually active women who do not use any method of contraception become pregnant in the course of one year.

There are many types of contraceptives. Some of them need to be prescribed by a doctor. These are

• The Pill—The active ingredients in the pill are like the hormones that naturally regulate the menstrual cycle. Taken once a day, the pill is one of the most effective antipregnancy methods available. Most birth-control pills keep the ovaries from releasing eggs. No eggs, no pregnancy. Others prevent pregnancy by changing the lining of the uterus so that if there is a fertilized egg, it can't get implanted. And some pills change the cervical mucus (moisture that comes out of the vagina) so that sperm can't move up there. Some of the advantages of the pill are:

1. It's convenient to use.
2. Women who use the pill have less menstrual flow, less cramping, more regular periods, and less acne.
3. Women who take the pill correctly every day have less than a 1 percent chance of getting pregnant during the first year of use.

Some of the problems that can occur while taking the pill are:

1. Breast tenderness
2. Nausea

3. Weight gain or loss
4. Breakthrough bleeding between periods

These side effects are usually short-lived.

Pill users also have a somewhat greater chance than nonusers of developing blood clots, liver problems, and heart attacks as they grow older. The risks are highest in women over 40, smokers, and in those who have high blood pressure or diabetes.

You need to find out from a doctor (either a private one or one at a clinic) whether one of the types of pills is right for you.

• **The IUD (intrauterine device)**—These small plastic devices with strings attached are made of plastic that contain copper or a hormone and are inserted in the uterus by a doctor. Some of them can be left in place for eight years. IUDs usually prevent fertilization of the egg. They may also work by affecting the way sperm or eggs move or by affecting the lining of the uterus in a way that prevents implantation of a fertilized egg. No implantation, no development of an embryo. Some of the advantages of wearing an IUD are:

1. It's convenient—the woman doesn't need to think about using her birth-control method every day or every time she has intercourse. If it works well for a woman,

there's only a 2 to 3 percent chance of getting pregnant during the first year of use.
2. An IUD doesn't change the hormone levels in the blood.

As with most birth-control methods, IUDs have some disadvantages:

1. For a short time after insertion, cramping might be greater, bleeding could occur between periods, and periods could be heavier and last longer.
2. It's possible for the IUD to fall out, and then pregnancy can occur.
3. The biggest problem has been that bacteria can move up the string attached to the IUD, which hangs out of the vagina. It can lead to pelvic inflammatory disease and sterility.

IUDs seem to work best for women who already have had a baby, as they stay in place better. They also work well for women who have only one sex partner who is having intercourse only with her because there's less chance of an infection moving up the string.

You have to see a doctor to find out which IUDs are available and whether it would be a good choice for you. At present, not too many doctors are prescribing the IUD.

• **The diaphragm and cervical cap**—These flexible rubber barriers fit securely in the vagina and cover the cervix. Both are best used with a spermicidal cream, foam, or jelly. The diaphragm is dome-shaped with a flexible rim that should fit well enough in the vagina to cover the cervical area. The cervical cap is thimble-shaped, smaller than the diaphragm, and fits very snugly over the cervix itself. Each of them blocks the entrance to the uterus, and the spermicidal cream, foam, or jelly used with them kills the sperm. No sperm, no pregnancy. The right size for you needs to be determined by a doctor or nurse practitioner. After you have a baby, you will need a larger size.

The diaphragm can be inserted up to 6 hours before intercourse and may be left in place for 24 hours. Each time intercourse is repeated, more jelly, cream, or foam must be inserted in the vagina without removing the diaphragm. The cervical cap may be left in place for up to 48 hours.

Advantages of these methods are:

1. Once learned, insertion is easy. Insertion can be part of a bedtime routine, or it can be shared by both partners during sex play.
2. The spermicide offers some protection against certain STDs, including AIDS.

Problems with these two devices include:

1. If they do not fit well, they can become dislodged. They might also be dislodged during some positions of intercourse—for example, when the woman is on top.
2. Some women are prone to develop bladder infections when using a diaphragm.
3. Women who have short fingers might need an inserter for putting in the diaphragm and might not be able to use a cervical cap at all.
4. An unpleasant odor might result if the cervical cap is worn for more than three days.
5. Some women have allergic reactions to the rubber, foam, cream or jelly.

Women who use the diaphragm or cervical cap have about an 18 percent chance of becoming pregnant during the first year of use. The failure rate increases if spermicidal cream, foam, or jelly are not used.

A doctor or other health practitioner will tell you whether or not you are a good candidate for either of these methods.

• **Depo-provera**—This relatively new birth-control method is a long-acting form of hormonal birth control and is given every 12 weeks by injection. It is very suitable for women who experience side effects from other methods or for whom other methods don't work.

• **Norplant**—This hormonal product consists of six thin capsules inserted under the skin of the upper arm. The capsules remain in place for five years.

Both Depo-provera and Norplant are more effective than either the pill or an IUD. Since these are very new methods, you would do well to consult a Planned Parenthood clinic to find out what its experience has been with them and whether these methods would be suitable for you.

Here are some methods which can be obtained over the counter, without needing a doctor or a clinic:

• **Condoms**—This birth-control device slips on over the erect penis and contains the sperm. It keeps sperm from getting into the vagina and from there into the uterus. Be sure to get the latex ones. There are some "skin" types which are supposed to give more sensitivity, but they do not keep out viruses. Also, for guys who boast that they are "too large" for ordinary condoms, there are now some new ones which are made for very big, or even for oddly shaped penises.

Recently, a female condom has been developed which looks like a large male condom with two rings on either end. One ring fits on the cervix, and the other fits over the vulva. It forms a receptacle to catch semen. There haven't been many reports about it yet because it is so new.

Advantages of male condoms are:

1. They allow men to take responsibility for birth control and STD prevention.
2. They have no side effects (except for the few people allergic to rubber or spermicide).
3. They are very easy to get and can be found at drugstores and at Planned Parenthood and other clinics.
4. They are a reliable backup or second method for the various female-birth-control methods.
5. They can be very sexy if your partner gets involved in putting it on and smoothing out the air bubbles.
6. They are the most effective means of preventing the transmission of AIDS and other STDs. For even greater safety, they should be used with a spermicide (nonoxynol 9 is recommended).

Some of the problems that may be associated with condom use are:

1. If not put on correctly, they can break. You must be sure to squeeze $1/2$ inch at the tip to eliminate any air bubbles and leave room for the semen.
2. If the guy doesn't hold the rim of the condom when he pulls out after climax, the contents can spill out into the vagina, raising the risk of pregnancy and STDs.
3. If the couple doesn't include condom use

in their love play together, putting on the condom can be an interruption.

4. Some guys say that feeling is reduced when condoms are used. (Others, however, say that condoms keep them from coming too soon.)

Using condoms, there is only a 12 percent chance of a pregnancy during the first year of use. Added protection can be achieved if, at the same time, a woman uses foam, cream, jelly, sponge, a diaphragm or a cervical cap. No matter what contraceptive a woman uses, if a man uses a latex condom at the same time, all risks are reduced.

• **Contraceptive foams, creams, jellies, suppositories, and sponges**—Foams, creams, jellies, and suppositories (capsules or films) are liquids or solids that melt and spread in the vagina after they are inserted. Sponges are soft, round, and about 2 inches in diameter. They are made of a solid synthetic substance. Each has a nylon loop attached to the bottom for easy removal. All of these are available over-the-counter at any drugstore.

All the above methods block the entrance to the uterus (cervix) and contain a spermicide that kills sperm. There is an 18 to 21 percent chance of pregnancy during the first year of use.

Advantages of over-the-counter methods are:

1. The spermicides, in addition to offering protection against pregnancy, also offer some protection against STDs.
2. They are easy to buy in most pharmacies and some supermarkets.
3. No prescriptions or fittings are needed.
4. Once learned, insertion is easy and may be done by your partner as part of sex play.

Some disadvantages of using over-the-counter methods are:

1. If not used exactly as directed, these products may not form a good barrier to the uterus. Some women complain of messiness or leakage.
2. Although rare, the spermicides in these methods may irritate the penis or vagina. Switching brands may solve this problem.
3. If left in more than 24 hours, users of the sponge may be at increased risk of toxic shock syndrome, which is also associated with the use of highly absorbent tampons.
4. Some women complain that the sponge is messy because it must be dipped in water before insertion. Others have complained that the sponge makes sex too dry.

The following are contraceptive procedures available to people who don't want to have any children or who feel they already have enough:

• Vasectomy—For men, the vasectomy consists of snipping the tubes (the vas deferens) that lead from the testes to the penis. If sperm can't get out of the testes, they can't get into the woman. No sperm, no babies.

• Tubal ligations—A kind of vasectomy for women, tubal ligations surgically pinch off the fallopian tubes, the passageways down which an egg travels in order to get fertilized. If the egg can't get down the tubes in order for sperm to get to it, no conception occurs.

There are two more methods not yet available in this country but highly effective in their use in Europe:

• RU 486 and the "morning-after" pill—Both are taken soon after unprotected intercourse and prevent a fertilized egg from being implanted in the uterus.

You may wish to explore in detail the many methods that are available for contraception. You can get all the information you want by calling or visiting any Planned Parenthood or Teen Clinic in your community.

As I said at the beginning of this chapter, the best form of contraception is not having intercourse at all. That doesn't mean you can't have fun sexually. Go ahead and caress and fondle each other. Mutually masturbate each other to orgasm. As long as you don't have intercourse, you don't

have to worry about unwanted pregnancy or
STDs.

Kids have lots of questions about contraception. Here are a few of them:

Q: Which is the best kind of condom for sensitivity?
A: All condoms are thin enough to afford plenty
of sensitivity. Some macho guys say, "I don't get
any feelings out of the condom. It's like taking a
shower with a raincoat on." But if two lovers engage in mutual stimulation, the guy will get
plenty of feeling, even while wearing a condom.
This sensitivity thing is highly exaggerated. I
think guys just don't want to go to the trouble to
learn how to use a condom sexily and effectively.
I sometimes say jokingly to guys, "If you're worried about sensitivity so much, wear two condoms all day, and when you have intercourse,
take one off." Also, putting a drop of water-based
spermicide down in the tip of the condom before
putting it on it will increase a guy's sensitivity.
Never use oil-based lubricants like Vaseline, mineral oil, or vegetable oil. They will destroy the
condom.

**Q: How common is it for a condom to tear during
intercourse and why?**
A: It is quite common if the condom is not used
properly. What I mean by "properly" is this:

• You must leave ½ inch at the end in order to get rid of air bubbles and catch the semen. Otherwise, the condom may break.

• You must hold on to the rim of the condom when you pull out because after ejaculation, the penis becomes flaccid (limp) and the condom can slip off. This will cause the semen to spill and perhaps get into the vagina, which means that sperm can swim up the uterus and fertilize the egg.

• When you unroll the condom onto the penis, be sure not to snag it or tear it with your nails.

• Be sure you're not using a condom you've been carrying around in your wallet for months or years. Old latex deteriorates and can break easily.

• Never use Vaseline or any other oil-based product with a condom. Use a water-based spermicide.

If all these precautions are taken, the condom shouldn't break, and sperm shouldn't spill.

Q: How can a teenage girl get the pill? Where does she go, and do her parents have to know?
A: Call any Planned Parenthood or Teen Clinic for an appointment. And bring your boyfriend with you because he should share in the experience. No, your parents don't have to know. These facilities always ensure confidentiality. If you can, however, it would be good to share your

choice with your parents. It would be nice if your parents could be proud of you for taking responsibility. Try to establish some mutual communication with them and show them that you're taking care of yourself. When making your birth-control decision, remember that the pill prevents pregnancy, but not the transmission of STDs.

Q: If you use birth control (the pill), does it endanger your fertility chances after you quit using it?
A: Sometimes, after going off the pill, it takes time for your body chemistry to get back to normal. But, for the most part, unless there was a problem before you went on the pill, it won't affect your fertility.

Q: How safe is the pill as a form of birth control?
A: If you get the pill from a doctor or practitioner who takes your medical history and prescribes the type and dosage that is best for you, then it is a very safe method. Also, doctors and practitioners always ask that you keep them informed of the effects you experience when taking the pill (such as painful breasts, breakthrough bleeding, weight gain, etc.) They can then see whether the prescription needs to be changed. Never take someone else's pills. A dosage that doesn't fit your particular needs can be harmful to your health.

Q: How do you use a douche?
A: I didn't even mention douching as a form of birth control because it is highly ineffective. It only takes a few seconds for sperm to move into the uterus, and douches don't reach high enough. It's pretty hard to douche quickly enough after unprotected intercourse to wash away the sperm from the vagina. Do not rely on this form of contraception.

Q: What time during a girl's cycle is it less likely for her to get pregnant?
A: Theoretically, it is safer just before, during, or just after menstruation because no eggs are supposed to be present at those times of the month. The most fertile time is supposed to be in the middle of your cycle, when ovulation occurs. Even if you have a very regular and predictable menstrual cycle, however, anytime you experience stress, get a cold, or get fatigued, your cycle can be thrown off without your even realizing it. I always tell young women to not rely on the so-called "safe period." Never have unprotected intercourse—it's a health hazard in more ways than one. Not only is there always the risk of unwanted pregnancy, but unprotected intercourse is a way to increase your risk of catching STDs.

Q: What is the best nonpermanent method—diaphragm, pills, etc.?
A: If you're talking about avoiding pregnancy

only, the most effective are the pill, Depo-provera, and Norplant. However, pregnancy is only one risk of unprotected intercourse. With the worry about AIDS these days, even if you go on the pill or another method, be sure to use condoms too. If, for some reason, you are unable to go on the pill, condoms alone, when used properly, are a very effective method, especially when used along with spermicidal creams, jellies or foam. A diaphragm, used with a spermicide, is another very good method.

Q: Do birth-control pills cause cancer?
A: Whenever hormones are introduced into the body, there is always some worry about cancer. Current research is trying to determine whether there is any relationship between the pill and breast cancer. So far, no one knows for sure. As far as cervical cancer is concerned, it appears that women on the pill are less prone to it than others. If there is a history of cancer in your family, especially breast cancer, it may not be a good idea to go on the pill. The practitioner or doctor you consult will take a full medical history and give you a complete exam to see if you are a good candidate for it.

Q: Can a man feel a diaphragm during sex?
A: Some men have reported that, when thrusting, they can feel the rim of the diaphragm. But its rare. A small number even report feeling the

string of an IUD. If it's irritating to the man, the couple should explore other means of contraception. Perhaps, the couple can find new positions or engage in more sexual playing to minimize the man's prolonged contact.

Q: What is the safest combination of birth control?
A: If you insist on having intercourse these days, the safest is for the man to wear a condom and the woman to take the pill or wear a diaphragm. You might also consider Norplant as an alternative to the pill.

Q: If you take the pill, how often should you take it?
A: The pill must be taken every day. You'll find out the entire procedure when you go to a clinic or doctor to get the pill that fits your particular needs. You will not only learn all about how to take the pill, but what to watch for while taking it. Remember: never take any pills that have not been prescribed for you alone.

Q: Is it OK to be on the pill at 16?
A: If you are having intercourse, and the pill has been prescribed by a doctor or practitioner, it is definitely OK. It is certainly better than getting pregnant at that age! To be sure you're protected against STDs, however, ask your boyfriend to wear a condom during intercourse, too.

Q: How do you approach buying a condom where you won't be nervous?
A: Many young people are nervous about buying condoms because they think they're doing something naughty by having sex and they worry that they will be looked at with disapproval. If you are planning to become sexually active with intercourse included, however, don't worry about criticism from others. Give yourself credit for wanting to be protected not only against unwanted pregnancy but also against STDs. I hope that pharmacists will realize that it is commendable for kids not to want to take risks. I believe that if you act with confidence, you will receive less criticism. What's more, these days, you don't really have to ask anyone at the counter to get condoms or spermicides for you. They are usually out on the shelves or right near the cash register. All you have to do is take one and pay for it—no explanation necessary.

Q: Is withdrawal a safe method?
A: It's better than nothing, and a lot of people use it when they have no other method but it's not a reliable method. The problem is that, before a guy comes, a fluid called the "pre-ejaculate" comes out of the penis. Although no one is sure about this, it might have enough sperm in it to cause a pregnancy. Also, if the guy is HIV-positive, there might be enough virus in the pre-ejaculate to transmit the virus.

Chapter 8
What's Normal?

Here in America, we are obsessed with normality. We do tests and research in order to determine what's normal and what's not, so we'll know whether we're normal. The final word seems to be that pretty much everything is normal somewhere in the world.

One of the things that is wonderful about human beings is that we are so different from one another. Whether it relates to food or clothing or sex, there are as many norms as there are people. What's normal is what is right for you that does no harm to others.

Because we have been a sexually repressed society, we focus a lot of our "normal" mania on sex and sexuality. Since we still don't have enough education about sexuality, we try to make one thing right and normal and everything else abnormal and wrong. In truth, if you look around the world, you'll often find that what is considered deviant in one place is considered perfectly acceptable in another. In our society, since we have a history which considered sex good only for reproduction, any activities solely for the sake of pleasure were seen as abnormal. This attitude still lingers today.

For example, here in America, masturbation is still considered dirty and bad. In some places, such as Malaysia, mothers routinely stimulate the genitals of irritable infants to orgasm to calm and comfort them. Just because we don't do that here doesn't mean it isn't normal in the human population.

Size is another topic we spend a lot of time establishing normalcy in—especially penis size. Many questions teenage boys ask me are about penis size. What's normal? Is bigger better? Does size matter? I always tell them that size doesn't matter. It's caring, attention to what turns you and your partner on, and a loving attitude that make the difference in lovemaking—not whether your penis is 10 inches long. Most women don't have orgasms through intercourse alone—it's the sexual playing that counts. If a young woman discovers for herself what gives her pleasure and then communicates that to her partner, she can have great orgasms along with that partner.

Undue attention to the size of penises and breasts is all in reaction to what is normal and what is not. In the case of penises and breasts, we want to establish what's normal so that we can strive for and boast about "supernormal"—giant breasts and huge penises. But bigger is not always better. Every size is normal.

Anatomically, every one of us is different. No two penises are exactly the same. No two clitorises are exactly the same. No two people like to be touched or kissed in exactly the same way. It's this great diversity that makes us so interesting as a species. And while it's true that a majority of people may have *similar* characteristics, no *one* way is the only way to be.

The same holds true of sexual orientation. Because there has been little education about homosexuality, many people see *it* and bisexuality as abnormal. You'll find out in Chapter 11 that homosexuality and bisexuality are as normal as heterosexuality.

In our haste to establish what is normal and what is not, we are preventing ourselves from experiencing the full spectrum of pleasure and plea-

suring. Anything sexual between consenting parties—as long as you do it safely and responsibly
and without exploitation—is normal. Here are
some questions teens have asked me about
what's normal:

**Q: Is masturbation normal for boys and girls dur-
ing the early teens and throughout life?**
A: Yes. As I've said before masturbation is normal
at every stage in life. Early in life, little children
discover the pleasure of touching themselves, and
they never forget it. Unfortunately, because we
are so uncomfortable with pleasuring, we make
ourselves feel guilty about masturbation. Many
people still consider masturbation dirty and sinful. It's not. Masturbation is normal whether you
do it or not. In fact, masturbation and mutual
masturbation are two of the safest sex activities
we can engage in. Not only does masturbation
provide an excellent outlet for sexual tension but,
as I've said throughout this book, it gives you the
opportunity to discover the most pleasure-inten-
sive spots on your body. Later on, when you have
a partner, you can share this knowledge with that
partner, both verbally and nonverbally.

Q: What is the average size of a male penis?
A: First of all, all penises are male, and all sizes
are normal. As many men as there are in the
world, there are that many different sizes. What's
more, the size and shape of the penis are not re-

lated to a man's body build, race, virility, or his ability to give and receive sexual satisfaction. It is thought that the obsession men have with large penises is related to an association with male fertility and power. That association isn't founded in fact. Any size penis can be fertile and powerful.

Q: Does a penis have to be a certain size for a girl to have an orgasm?
A: No. A guy's penis size is not related to a girl's orgasm. There are all different size penises and vaginas just as there are different size noses, arms, and legs. Because the vagina is a strong, elastic organ, it can accommodate a penis of almost any size. Besides, the size of the penis is not the important thing in lovemaking. Caring, attentiveness to pleasuring, and respect for your partner's individuality are really the important things in lovemaking. If you truly care about your partner's pleasure and pay attention to the kind of touching and caressing that excite her the most, the size of your penis will have little to do with helping her achieve orgasm. Using your fingers, mouth and maybe even a vibrator is often far more effective than the penis-in-vagina method.

Q: Why do girls smell like tuna fish down there?
A: Every human has his or her own individual odor. This applies to genital smell as well. Healthy, clean female genitals should not have an offensive odor. If there is an offensive odor, and a

strong fishy smell, it could mean a trichomonas infection. Have it checked. It's easily treatable.

It's usually a good idea for playful sexual partners to wash their genitals well before sex play and, in fact, showering or bathing together and washing each other's genitals can be very exciting.

Q: If a girl doesn't have sex for more than two months, does her hole get smaller?
A: No. Vaginas come in all different sizes and widths, and they remain that way under normal circumstances. It's true that you can stretch the vaginal tissue if large objects are inserted on a regular basis. It's also true that, in some cases, if a woman is extremely afraid of sex, the entrance to her vagina may contract so that not even a finger can fit in. Medical treatment over a short period of time with different size inserters, and counseling about the cause of the fear, will stretch the entrance and correct the condition.

Also, after childbirth, vaginas widen from the great expansion that occurs to permit the baby to emerge. But the width of the vagina has very little to do with sexual pleasuring because the vagina has very few nerve endings. Girls can derive more pleasure from massaging the entrance to the vagina and the clitoris. Also, rubbing and caressing their breasts and different skin areas often produce more pleasure than inserting anything into the vagina.

Q: When will my breasts grow?

A: Girls' breasts grow at different rates and to different sizes. Breasts can start to grow as early as age 8 and as late as age 18. It all depends on when your individual hormone system kicks in. There's no normal breast-growth age. There's no normal breast size either. Some girls remain flat-chested all their lives. Some grow big breasts quite young. Breast size has nothing to do with getting pleasure from sex. Small breasts are as sensual as big ones. Our society's focus on big breasts is silly. It makes girls think that guys are interested only in girls whose breasts are big. That's not true. We humans have many different tastes. And there's someone out there who will think the size of your breasts is perfect.

Q: How come I get turned on why my girlfriend rubs my neck?

A: Because, other than our brains, the skin is our largest sex organ. Our skin is filled with nerve endings that send pleasure shooting into our brains when we are touched by someone special. Whether you're a boy or a girl, you can be turned on by a massage from either a boy or a girl, and it's perfectly normal. Besides, people have different clusters and locations of nerve endings on their skin. Some people have reported orgasms from having their faces, necks, or breasts massaged. Others adore foot massage. It's fun to explore slowly with a partner what parts of your skin excite you.

Q: What's a wet dream?
A: When boys have sexual dreams, they often get so stimulated that they get erections in their sleep and ejaculate. That's a wet dream. Wet dreams are normal. They are most common in teenage boys. Hormones are raging through their bloodstreams. Everything turns them on. Even in their sleep, they're fantasizing about sex. Don't worry. You can always wash your sheets. Incidentally, girls experience nocturnal orgasms in their sleep as well. They just don't ejaculate.

Q: What do you think of breast implants?
A: Breast implants are a direct result of our society's obsession with big breasts. Somehow we equate bigger with better. The bigger the breast, the more sexual it is considered. Not true. Small breasts are just as sexy as big breasts. And breasts that have no implants are more sensitive to stimulation than breasts with implants. What's more, it has recently been found that silicone breast implants can be dangerous. If the silicone escapes into your body, it can make you very sick. Breast implants may turn hard over the years and can be very painful. As long as you remember that every size breast is normal and sensitive, and that there's someone out there who will appreciate your breasts for what they are, you don't have to

buy the myth that bigger is better. It's true that some guys have an infantile attraction to huge breasts, but what has that got to do with a good loving relationship?

Q: What if a boy can't get an erection?
A: Not getting an erection is pretty normal. Not every guy gets an erection every time. And an erection is not critical to sexual pleasure. In fact, if a guy is scared or nervous for any reason, occasionally he might not be able to get an erection. However, if he doesn't focus on the erection and simply pays attention to other kinds of sexual pleasuring, his partner will love it and he'll be so turned on that his worries will diminish. That, in itself, will usually lead to an erection.

Quadriplegics who cannot get erections still achieve a psychic release that's just like an orgasm and can bring their partners to orgasm using manual and oral stimulation.

Of course, if you find that you *never* can get an erection, it would be a good idea to check with a doctor or a psychologist.

Q: Does the first time hurt?
A: It's pretty normal for girls to experience pain the first time they have sex. The vagina is tight and not used to having large objects, like penises, inserted in it. What's more, the hymen—a piece of tissue stretched across the vaginal opening—is often torn the first time a penis is introduced into

the vagina. This can cause some pain and even a little bleeding. These days, however, girls are so physically active (horseback riding, gymnastics, bike riding, and so forth), and use tampons that the hymen is usually torn long before they have intercourse.

Often, when a girl has sex for the first time, she tenses up. This can cause pain, too. Remember, you don't need insertion to achieve sexual pleasure. In fact, sexual pleasure might be easier and better without insertion. Eventually her tension will disappear.

Q: Why do boys like sex more than girls?
A: Conditioning. For years, girls have been taught to repress their sexuality because sexually active girls simply weren't accepted. They had to be pure, demure, and virginal. Boys, on the other hand, have always been encouraged to flaunt their sexuality and enjoy it. Even today, if a girl admits she likes sex, she's often called a slut or a whore, so she tends to hold back. But if a guy boasts about a lot of sex, he's admiringly called a stud.

It's perfectly normal for a girl to desire sexual pleasure as much as a guy. It doesn't make her loose or a slut. If boys and girls learn to pleasure each other without intercourse, there's no reason why a girl can't enjoy sex as much as a boy without the fear of becoming pregnant. Also, boys will find they can double their fun if they slow down and focus on prolonging pleasure for their partners instead of taking the "wham, bam, thank you, ma'am" speed approach. If a guy ever criticizes you for admitting that you enjoy your sexuality, dump him!

Q: Is it OK to be a virgin at 17?
A: If by virgin you mean never having had intercourse, it's not only OK, it could be great. Intercourse is highly overrated. It's a real health hazard. You can have far more pleasure (and better lover training) by engaging in fantasy and friction (masturbation) or mutual sexual play to orgasm (mutual masturbation) with a partner. It doesn't matter at what age you become sexually involved, as long as you act safely and responsibly. Everyone starts at a different time. Everyone is ready at a different time. And intercourse is only a part of it that might better be saved for possibly having babies with the person you want to stay with for a long time.

Q: How old do you have to be to stop having sex?
A: There's no normal age to stop having sex as long as you recognize that "having sex" doesn't necessarily mean only intercourse. People are sexual from before birth until death. While your sex drive slows up (like everything else in your body) as you get older, you never stop wanting to be pleasured by or wanting to give pleasure to another human being. And there's no reason why

you can't continue to be sexually active as long as you live. That includes self-pleasuring if you don't have a partner.

Q: Can you tell me about autoerotic asphyxiation?
A: Autoerotic asphyxiation is a dangerous activity that has killed many kids, mainly boys. It isn't acceptable sexual behavior because it is self-exploitive. Someone discovered that during masturbation when you're just about to come, if you cut off your oxygen by tightening a rope or a tie around your neck, your orgasm is stronger. The trouble is, when you're having an orgasm, you're not in total control. You often forget about the rope, cut off all your oxygen and die. NEVER try autoerotic asphyxiation. A plain old orgasm is fantastic all by itself!

Chapter 9
What about Oral Sex?

O ral sex means pleasuring a man by sucking or licking his penis and/or scrotum, or pleasuring a woman by licking or sucking her clitoris or vaginal area. It can also include licking the anal area of either partner. The technical term for sucking male genitals is "fellatio." The technical term for sucking female genitals is "cunnilingus." There are lots of slang words for this, too: "going down on," "giving head," "blowjob," "sixty-nine" and "eating," to name just a few. The term I prefer is "genital kissing." The term for oral-anal stimulation is "rimming."

I always get a lot of questions from teens about oral sex. And it's no surprise. Nowhere in our society or in schools is this subject discussed seriously. There's no unit on oral sex in sex-education courses. Oral sex is often considered dirty, smelly, and somehow deviant. Naturally, this provokes a high degree of interest in the topic. And because factual information is not readily accessible, teens get their information where they can. Therefore, a lot of *mis*information is passed on. Misconceptions and mythology are perpetuated. Teens have few places to find out the truth.

The truth is that oral sex is not gross or bad— provided it's done responsibly, safely, and caringly. Oral sex is a direct outgrowth of our boundless adventurousness. Human beings are explorers of the senses: touch, taste, smell, sight, and hearing. We use our hands, lips, tongues, noses, eyes, ears, and all other parts of our bodies to enhance our contact with our world. Take food, for example. We not only taste what we eat, we admire its appearance, we smell it, we touch it, we listen to its crunch, we roll it around inside our mouths to savor every tasty bit.

It's the same with sexuality. When oral sex is performed by two people who care about themselves and each other, it can be a delicious and total sensory experience for both, as well as a safe alternative to intercourse.

It's important for all you readers to recognize that I'm speaking about oral sex between two people who do not carry the AIDS virus. If any oral sex is indulged in with anyone whose AIDS condition is not known, protect yourself: use a condom or a dental dam. To find out more about AIDS and how it's transmitted, see Chapter 6.

It's not perverted to be interested in oral sex. Here are a few questions I've been asked about this subject:

Q: If you swallow sperm or come, is it harmful?
A: No. In fact, *healthy* semen is full of protein with a little bit of sugar. It's fun to know that the sugar is called fructose. However, for various psychological reasons based on the perception in our society that everything "down there" is dirty, some people find it difficult to swallow. But it won't hurt you.

Q: Can a girl get pregnant if she gets sperm in her mouth?
A: No. Girls can get pregnant only if sperm get into their vaginas and swim up the fallopian tubes to fertilize an egg.

Q: Why do people eat pussy?
A: First of all, let's define pussy. Pussy is another

word for the female genitals. "Eating pussy" is another term for oral sex, or cunnilingus. People do it because it really excites both them and their partners. When you care about your partner, you care about what turns them on. And when they're turned on, so are you.

Q: Why would anyone want to have oral sex?
A: Some people use oral sex as a substitute for intercourse to avoid pregnancy. But mostly people do it because of its great orgasmic potential. There are nerve endings all over both the male and female genitals which react with great pleasure when stimulated by a warm, moist tongue and mouth. Licking and sucking are very effective for producing powerful orgasms.

Q: How many calories are there in oral sex?
A: I haven't seen a single study on this but I doubt the number is significant. If you're really worried about gaining weight, just don't eat any candy on days you have oral sex with your partner.

Q: Is oral sex normal?
A: Yes. Anything that pleasures you and your partner, as long as it doesn't harm either one, is normal. Humans exhibit a wide range of normal sexual behavior, and oral sex falls right on that spectrum. Some uninformed people think of oral sex as something that only homosexuals engage in, but that's not true. It's something that most

humans engage in as a normal pleasurable behavior.

Q: What does it feel like to get head from a girl?
A: It obviously feels great because so many guys want it.

Q: Do a lot of diseases get transmitted through oral sex?
A: Sexually transmitted diseases (STDs) can be passed along through oral sex. For example, if a male partner is HIV-positive and you engage in oral sex and he ejaculates into your mouth, you can also become HIV-positive if you've got cuts or abrasions in your mouth. Some diseases, like herpes simplex I (cold sores) can be transmitted through oral sex, too. Sometimes a simple cold sore can appear in the genital area. In a small number of cases, a cold sore in the mouth area can mutate into herpes simplex II in the genital area. That can be a bit more serious. And if someone has genital herpes and there are any lesions on the genitals or anus, they can be transmitted to the mouth through oral sex. Genital herpes is easy to cure and is not life threatening.

STD transmission can be prevented by condoms on guys or a rubber dam on girls. The rubber dam is the same kind used by your dentist to isolate a tooth during a procedure, so it's usually called a dental dam. It's a latex rectangle that can be stretched over the vaginal area. It's thin

141

enough to allow total sensory input and no germ output. Since these dams are not always easy to find, you can split a condom down its side and open it up to make a homemade dam.

Q: What is sixty-nine?
A: A couple may engage in mutual genital kissing simultaneously. This is called "69" because, when you think of it, the two bodies are positioned just like those numbers.

Q: What are the risks of sixty-nine?
A: The risks of sixty-nine are transmitting sexual diseases.

Q: What is a blowjob?
A: A blowjob is a sexual practice that involves one person placing a partner's penis in his or her mouth and sucking and licking until the partner achieves orgasm. Sometimes the penis is removed from the mouth before orgasm. Sometimes ejaculation occurs in the mouth. It really is a misnomer to call it a "blow" job because no blowing is going on.

Q: What if a girl gives a guy a blowjob and he goes to the bathroom in her mouth?
A: That would be gross but, most of the time, it wouldn't be dangerous. Urine is not poisonous. It rarely happens because the urinary bladder is closed off when an erection occurs.

142

Q: Can a girl get sick if she gives a boy a blowjob?
A: Yes. STDs can be transmitted this way if a condom is not used. Girls can get sick in another way, too. Some girls get disgusted by semen because they don't know anything about it, so they might feel nauseated.

Q: When a girl gives you a blowjob, can she pop a vein in your dick?
A: Only if her suction power is superhuman. I don't think there's a single recorded case of a girl popping a vein in a guy's penis because she gave him a blowjob.

Q: When a girl is giving you a blowjob, can she bite you?
A: Sure, if she wants to, and I'm sure it would hurt quite a bit; but I guess she'd have to be a pretty hostile person to want to hurt you. If that happened, you would definitely have to examine the relationship! Another thing—I don't think there are many recorded cases of girls biting guys' dicks *off* during blowjobs.

Q: Can a boy give himself a blowjob?
A: Only if he's a yoga master. That would require quite a bit of flexibility! A hand job is much easier for a boy to give himself.

Q: Does a blowjob excite a man?
A: Yes. And so does cunnilingus. In fact, recent

research shows that teenage boys enjoy both fellatio and cunnilingus more than girls.

Q: What do you think of oral sex before marriage?
A: I think it's a good alternative to intercourse. A lot of girls feel that way, too, because it means they don't have to worry about getting pregnant. Some teenage girls, however, refuse to engage in oral sex even if they've already had intercourse because they see that as a much more intimate behavior than intercourse and would rather wait until they're with someone they really love.

Q: Why do some people find oral sex so repulsive?
A: Many kids worry about smells, particularly of the female genitals. If a person is healthy and clean, there is always a characteristic personal scent, but it isn't foul. Bad odors are caused by the bacteria that accumulate on unwashed bodies. All you have to do is bathe to get rid of any odors. In fact, showering or taking a bath together with your partner can be a wonderful and seductive prelude to lovemaking.

Another thing people find repulsive is swallowing semen or getting urine in their mouths. While this may seem gross, if the boy is healthy, neither of these fluids will cause any harm. Semen is mostly protein with a little sugar to energize the sperm. Urine is predominantly water with some salts added. In healthy people, it's totally harmless. Another thing: When a boy has an erection or is ejaculating, he usually can't urinate at the same time. In general, the penis can only do one thing at a time.

Q: Is fellatio or cunnilingus against the law?
A: Yes, in some states. However, such laws are not usually enforced because, for the most part, we believe that what people do in private is strictly their own business.

Q: Is there something wrong if you are not sexually stimulated by actual intercourse? I love oral sex, but intercourse just leaves me cold. I almost fall asleep. Is this normal?
A: Yes, this is quite normal. With oral sex, the sensitive parts of the genital area are far more deliberately and subtly stimulated than through intercourse. In fact, research shows that most women do not experience orgasm through intercourse alone. It's the sexual play that creates most of the pleasure, whether or not intercourse is included.

Q: Should you swallow or spit?
A: There's no "should" on this subject. People have different tastes. Neither swallowing nor spitting out is harmful, although swallowing may be considered sexier to a guy.

Q: Does the taste of semen vary with diet?
A: It can because digested foods are carried all

over the body by the circulatory system to provide nutrition for all the cells. Certain foods have
strong elements that may produce strong odors.
For example, when you eat garlic or onions, your
breath can smell of them. Or if you eat asparagus,
your urine takes on a strong smell. Beets can turn
your urine pink. Semen can also be affected but, if
the guy is healthy, it won't hurt you and
shouldn't be offensive.

**Q: Is it OK for a boy to go down on a girl while
she's got her period?**
A: If the girl is healthy, it's messy but not harmful. Sometimes it tastes bitter, but if a girl wears a
diaphragm while menstruating, very little of the
blood will seep down. If the girl is HIV-positive,
there's a risk of transmitting the disease through
contact with the menstrual blood and lubrication,
as explained in Chapter 6.

**Q: Do you think there's anything wrong with oral
sex?**
A: I don't, but everyone has a different opinion.
Whether or not people enjoy oral-genital or oral-
anal sex is a matter of preference and should not
be taken for granted. The subject needs to be
talked about by both partners and explored together, never imposed. If two people are mutually
willing to investigate pleasuring, they can certainly find the approaches that turn them on.

Q: If you wanted to go down on a guy, how would you approach him?
A: Once you become sexually intimate with someone, necking and petting are a good start. Once your clothes are off, gradually kissing all over the body and leading to oral sex is perfectly natural. Both partners, not just the male, should expect pleasuring to orgasm. One-way pleasuring is okay only within a mutual caring relationship where each person cares about the pleasuring of him/herself and the partner. Then, they can decide when to engage in one-way play and when to engage in two-way play.

Q: If you kiss someone's butt, is that oral sex?
A: If someone licks or kisses a partner's anal area, it is called "rimming" and is part of the overall category of oral sex. Since the entrance to the anus has many nerve endings, many people enjoy being stimulated there. I recommend that people use dental dams when engaging in that practice to avoid getting viruses or bacteria in the mouth. If partners kiss or gently bite each other on the buttocks, that isn't oral sex. It's just sexual playing.

Chapter 10
What about Anal Sex?

Anal sex is the practice of penetrating the anus for sexual pleasure. It is one of the highest-risk sexual behaviors you can engage in.

The anus is made up of a very thin layer of tissue, the surface of which is covered with a lot of blood vessels. This tissue can be easily torn when a large object is introduced, resulting in bleeding.

This leads to a high risk of transmission of AIDS. Remember that in order for the AIDS virus to be passed from one infected individual to another, two conditions have to be met:

1. A large enough dose of the virus has to be present.
2. There has to be a blood connection.

If an HIV-positive male has unprotected anal sex with a noninfected person, his semen would have a large dose of the virus. And if the anal tissue should tear, the virus can be passed right into the bloodstream.

Anal sex is not just practiced by homosexual men. Many girls, unaware of the AIDS risks connected with it, use anal sex as a means of birth control. There's nothing wrong with anal sex, as long as it's done responsibly and safely.

Here are a few questions kids have asked me about anal sex:

Q: Can you get a girl pregnant through anal sex?
A: No. In order for a girl to get pregnant, the sperm has to enter the vagina, travel up the uterus to the fallopian tube, and fertilize an egg. The anus does not connect to the uterus in any way.

Q: Can you have anal intercourse face to face?
A: Yes, if you're talking about anal sex using the

penis. Many people's bodies are flexible enough so they can, indeed, have anal sex when they are face to face. When two men are lovers, if they like anal sex, they can do it face to face, but only one at a time. It would be nearly impossible to do it simultaneously. In the case of two women if they wanted to experience anal penetration, they'd need to use fingers or vibrators and could probably manage it simultaneously face to face. As a matter of fact, any type of couple could also use fingers and vibrators and try it face to face, if they so desired.

Q: Will anal sex hurt?
A: It can. The anus is not very elastic. The forcible introduction of any object can cause tearing and pain. That's why it is strongly recommended that a lubricant be used and that penetration be done gently. In that way pain and tearing can be avoided.

Q: Why do people engage in anal sex?
A: Because the entrance to the anus has many nerve endings, so there's sexual pleasure to be derived from it.

Q: It has been said that anal sex is directly related to AIDS. Why, then, do homosexuals continue to participate in the activity, knowing they could be endangering others?
A: Anal sex is related to AIDS because the anal

tissue is thin and has so many blood vessels. Homosexual men are not the only people who engage in anal sex. Anyone who gets into a lot of sexual exploration with a male partner will probably give or receive it sometime. However, an HIV-positive person who does it without protection could put any partner—gay or straight—at risk. That's irresponsible. Many homosexual men use condoms. Many heterosexuals use condoms, too. As long as a condom is used during anal intercourse, the risk of AIDS transmission is reduced. Of course, there are a lot of irresponsible people who either don't care about their fellow human beings or who get heavily into drugs and alcohol and lose all sense of responsibility. They are a danger to others, so *you* have to be sure to take care of yourself!

Q: Is anal sex OK?
A: Yes. Any sexual practice is OK as long as it is done by two consenting individuals and no one is harmed or exploited.

Chapter 11
What about Being Gay?

Homosexuality is the love of one man for another man or one woman for another woman. Usually homosexual men are referred to as "gays," while homosexual women are called "lesbians." Bisexuality is the ability to love people of either sex.

Homosexuals and bisexuals have been around as long as humans have. In fact, there is a great deal of historical, anthropological, biological, and psychological evidence showing that they fall within the normal range of human sexual expression. There are even documented instances of homosexual behavior in other animals.

Many famous people in our collective cultures have been gay: Oscar Wilde, Rudolf Nureyev, Martina Navratilova, Gertrude Stein, Rock Hudson, Lily Tomlin, Liberace, Leonard Bernstein, k.d. lang, Melissa Etheridge, Elton John, Rita Mae Brown, Dorothy Allison, Bob Mould, and many others. So why in the world are we so afraid of homosexuality, and why do we make such a big deal about it? Because of our heterosexual bias, stemming from the old norm. That's why.

Long ago, when our survival was by no means guaranteed, pronatalism—placing a top priority on procreating our species to ensure our continuation on this planet—was vital. Therefore, the heterosexual imperative for intercourse took precedence over other forms of sexual behavior. There were undoubtedly homosexual and bisexual people at the dawn of humankind, but if they were not productive in the reproductive sense, they may not have been prized. Still, some cultures have accepted even exclusive homosexuals as part of their society. Many have not. Cultures differ considerably in the way they handle anything, including sexuality.

We all have a basic instinctive drive for procreation; that is, reproduction. However, that's a biological imperative, and not our conscious motivation. Our conscious motivation, given to us by evolution (or God, if you prefer) is a psychological drive for pleasure seeking. And that's what human beings are looking for: pleasure. Sexually speaking, people all around the world and throughout history have found pleasure in countless ways: opposite-sex partners, same-sex partners, manual or mechanical stimulation etc. In responding to such a strong drive for pleasuring, there will be enough male-female sexual intercourse to ensure reproduction.

In the seventies, although polls showed that most Americans thought homosexuality was abnormal, many more options developed for gays and lesbians. They experienced more acceptance legally, socially, in employment, and in religion. Laws were passed barring discrimination against people simply because of their sexual orientation.

Then came AIDS—and a major about-face in the public consciousness. Since gay men were the first to contract AIDS, and had the greatest number of cases, they became a convenient scapegoat. Many people blamed gay men for the spread of the disease. Some extremists in the religious Right even say that AIDS is God's punishment for being homosexual. Nonsense! To prove that it's nonsense, you just have to think of lesbians, who are also homosexual and who have the lowest incidence, among all groups of people, of AIDS and every other sexually transmitted disease.

The beauty of being human is that we can experience a wide range of sexual pleasure and feelings. I like to say that humans are omnisexual. If we can get away from saying that one kind of attraction is right and another wrong, we could all try all kinds of safe sexuality. Then, we'd be less fearful and more tolerant.

That doesn't mean that everyone *has* to try every kind of sexual pleasuring that exists. You don't have to do anything you don't want to do. But you would be free to try what you wanted without having to worry about being called "queer."

It's normal to be curious about homosexuality in our society because we aren't taught anything about it anywhere in our education. I am constantly asked, "What causes homosexuality?"

Nobody knows for sure what causes someone to be homosexual or bisexual—or heterosexual, for that matter. To begin with, all human traits are determined by a genetic blueprint. That blueprint provides each of us with a range of potential in everything from musical talent, to height, to mathematics, to sexuality. The environment you grow up in determines whether or not you'll reach your full potential in any of your traits. Each trait has an upper and a lower limit of potential. Thank goodness we don't know our upper limit because that gives us the opportunity, the hope, and the desire to explore and learn, in order to reach our individual capabilities.

In terms of sexual orientation, there's a range of potential as well. I like to call the various possibilities "The Hacker Sexual Continuum." It is based on research Kinsey did in the 1940s and 1950s on thousands of subjects. He came up with a scale from 0 to 6. Zero represents people who are exclusively heterosexual, and 6 represents those who are exclusively homosexual. Numbers 1 to 5 represent all others in between who have both homosexual and heterosexual inclinations to one degree or another.

Here's what the Hacker Continuum looks like:

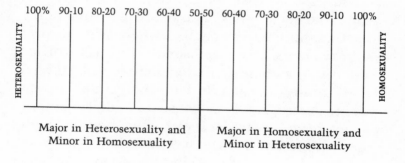

The continuum shows that we have varying strengths of sexual orientation, from being exclusively homosexual to being exclusively heterosexual, with all sorts of combinations and variations in between. As you can see, in the middle there's the 50/50 group who can function either heterosexually or homosexually. On either side of the 50/50 group, there are lots of people whom I say are majoring in homosexuality and minoring in heterosexuality and vice versa. Everyone falls on the continuum somewhere, and where you fall is determined by your genetic blueprint. Your environment determines how you act on your genetic blueprint. Whether or not you reach the unknown upper limit you're born with depends on chance, effort, and opportunity.

The Hacker Continuum does not place a value on where you fall. It isn't better to be 50/50, any other percentage, or all hetero or all homo. Wherever you find yourself on the continuum is fine and normal.

Kids are worried about being homosexual because our society is so homophobic (scared of homosexuality). Occasionally, when kids suspect they're not exactly heterosexual, they get worried and find it so hard to find anyone to talk to, that they commit suicide. In fact, the painful sexual-identity struggle is a cause of suicide among many teens. Instead of worrying, find an adult you admire and to whom you can disclose your fears. Ask about counselors or support groups that can help you discover and accept your identity.

Here are just a few of the questions that teens ask me about homosexuality:

Q: Why are there fags?
A: Why are there blacks? Why are there Chinese? Why are there dwarfs? Homosexuals are just part of the vast spectrum of different types of humans

we have on this planet. And it's the diversity of our population that makes us so interesting. Each group contributes something to the overall species picture and no one group is better—or worse —than the other. And it's better not use the word "fag" anymore. It has been such a nasty label. Let's adopt the motto, "It's not OK to be anti-gay!"

Q: How do you become a queer?
A: First, let's not use the word "queer." That implies wrongness. Let's say instead "homosexual." Once you have accepted that you fall somewhere on the Hacker Continuum genetically, then you can ultimately figure out how you might be inclined to express your sexuality. You might have a relationship with someone of the same sex, someone of the opposite sex, or both. You don't have to make any decision now. And you don't have to stick to a decision once you have made it. As you grow up, you need to be in tune with what kinds of people excite you the most and how you will choose to express your sexuality in a caring way. Here's a story that will illustrate what freedom of choice we all have:

Recently, a widow of 75 got some media attention because, after being married for 50 years, having five children and being widowed, she openly entered into a lesbian relationship which made her quite happy. There was naturally a lot of hoohah over what "caused" her to "turn into" a homosexual at such an advanced age. Nothing caused her to *turn into one.* Clearly, she had always had the potential (the genetic blueprint) for such feelings but had never explored them before. In interviews, she revealed that her marriage had been happy, but that she had always had fantasies about love and sex with another woman. Not until she was 75 did her environment give her the opportunity to act on these feelings. Without knowing her history, the strength of her fantasies, or the level of sexual satisfaction with her husband, it's hard to know where she fits on the Hacker Continuum. Maybe somewhere in the middle, quite close to the 50/50 mark.

Q: Is it OK when a girl thinks about another girl?
A: Yes, it's OK. In fact, it's normal, especially when you're a teenager. As a teenager, your hormones are raging. You get turned on by everything: the opposite sex, the same sex, music, maybe even cheeseburgers. Because we live in a society that has a fear of homosexuality, when young people have sexual feelings about someone of the same sex, they get scared. They think they're gay, and they get worried sick. That's because we are not taught anything about homosexuality or bisexuality in school. All these feelings are very normal, and there's no real way to tell what your sexual orientation is until you grow up. What's more, you can have same-sex fantasies without acting on them.

Q: How do lesbians have sex?
A: Any number of ways. Like heterosexuals, there isn't just one way for lesbians to make love to one another. Like heterosexuals, lesbians often start by kissing each other. Sometimes they put their tongues into one another's mouths. Touching and kissing each other's breasts is a big turn-on, too. Lesbians excite each other by rubbing each other's clitorises with their hands or using their tongues to tickle and stimulate their partners to orgasm. Vaginal penetration is done using fingers and, sometimes, a dildo. Each lesbian couple develops its own way of pleasuring each other.

Q: How do gays express sexual affection?
A: By gays, we generally mean homosexual men. Gays express affection by touching each other, hugging each other, kissing each other. When gay men have sex, they kiss and engage in mutual masturbation using their hands or mouths on their partner's penis to bring about orgasm. Anal sex may also be engaged in. It's a mistake to believe that anal sex is exclusive to homosexuals. Because it is a pleasurable activity, numerous individuals, regardless of orientation, use it for pleasuring. Except for vaginal intercourse, it is hard to identify any sexual behavior as belonging exclusively to homosexuals, bisexuals, or heterosexuals.

Q: I find that I am more attracted to other males. What do I do?
A: Find other males who are attracted to you. There's nothing wrong with being attracted to a guy if you're a guy. If you want to act on your attraction, you'll have to *carefully* feel out how other guys feel, to see whether they're interested in your advances. I use the word "carefully" because, in our society, it's best to be sure that the feelings are mutual before you act. Otherwise you may put yourself in a grave danger of being physically hurt. Also, if you're in high school, I do not recommend that you reveal your orientation right away. Because of a lack of education, teens are very hostile toward any evidence of homosexuality. Therefore, they can be very cruel and cause you a great deal of unhappiness. I recommend that you try to find a support group of young people with whom you can talk about your feelings. There are more and more of such groups springing up around the country to help young people who think they might be gay or bisexual.

If you don't want to act on your feelings, fantasizing about other guys is perfectly normal, and you can almost always engage in "fantasy and friction" (masturbation) as an outlet. If you don't want to fantasize about it, don't. You can always choose to act heterosexually if you also have that inclination. That doesn't mean, of course, that you'll stop being attracted to other males. It just means you choose not to express it outwardly.

Q: I think I'm gay. Is it wrong to be gay? People call me a homo.

A: It isn't wrong to be gay, but it can be difficult in our society. However, homophobia is just one of the ways fearful people have of blaming someone else for the variations in human behavior which they don't understand and which make them feel threatened. People who call you a homo, a fag, or a queer are just showing you how rigid and prejudiced they are. If we could get away from labeling people, we would learn that probably many people are capable of both homosexuality and heterosexuality to one degree or another. In a few American Indian tribes, the duality of human nature was recognized, and a person known as a "berdache" (someone who sometimes dressed and lived as a man and sometimes as a woman—no doubt a bisexual, to one degree or another) held a position of honor. Such recognition has also existed in other cultures and still does.

Q: Why are some people attracted to the same sex?

A: You might as well ask why some people are artists or why some people are taller than others. It's in their genetic blueprint to begin with. Somewhere in their DNA is one or a number of genes that say: "You feel sexually turned on by the same sex as you are." Whether or not people act on this genetic code depends on where on the

Hacker Continuum they fall, what culture they live in, and what experience they run into in life.

Q: How does someone decide whether or not they are homosexual?
A: You don't really decide whether or not you're homosexual. You decide whether or not you'll act on whatever percentage of homosexuality you happen to have. My friend Brian McNaught, a speaker and published author in the field of homosexuality, thinks there's a difference between sexual orientation, sexual identity, and sexual behavior. Sexual *orientation* is something you don't choose and can't change. Your genetic blueprint determines where you fall on the Hacker Continuum. Remember you can major in hetero and minor in homo, or vice versa. You can also be exclusively homo or hetero.

Sexual *identity* is the way you openly identify yourself, the self you present to the public. You can change your sexual identity. People who call themselves homosexuals and find that they're getting beaten up a lot might decide to change what they call themselves.

Sexual *behavior* is what kind of sexual activity you engage in: e.g., oral sex, anal sex, vaginal sex. Except for vaginal intercourse, there are no sexual behaviors that belong exclusively to any one sexual orientation. Behavior can also be changed. You might decide to eliminate anal sex for a while since it's a high-risk activity that can spread AIDS, if practiced without lubrication and a condom. You might also want to postpone intercourse until you decide whether or not you want to have children.

Here's a story to illustrate my point about identity:

A former student of mine felt relieved after hearing my lectures on the continuum of sexual orientation. In college he was in an intimate relationship with a man. But in high school, he had been in love with a young woman. He told me that when he graduates from college, he'd like to develop his career and then marry and have a family later in life. It would seem that he is very close to 50/50 on the continuum and has a choice about his sexual identity and behavior.

As I said in the chapter on love, when he marries, even though he will undoubtedly still have sexual yearnings for men, he will have to make a decision. I think that once you make a commitment to anyone, of any gender, you need to be exclusive. If the sexual fireworks get weaker as the relationship ages, you can work to revive them. Cheating is exploitative. So, if he wants to explore the other side of his sexuality, he will have to be honest with his wife about it. A few wives do not mind if their husbands occasionally act on their homosexual inclinations. However, that needs to be negotiated! And, in this era of AIDS, it could be very dangerous to the whole family. Sex is complex. I feel that if you have a good relationship, it is not necessary to satisfy every desire you ever have. In today's society, we never seem to have enough; and sometimes, in seeking more and more gratification, we go over the edge. This is definitely a health hazard whether it be connected with sex, alcohol, or drugs.

Q: If you have been with quite a few people of the opposite sex but were never really excited by them, is that a sign of homosexuality?
A: It could be. But it could also mean that you just haven't found the right heterosexual partner yet. The only way for you to tell is to be with someone of the same sex and see if the excitement is there. If it is, enjoy it—safely and responsibly, of course. If it isn't, you'll just have to wait until someone good for you comes along, regardless of gender.

Q: Do you approve of gayety? I don't.
A: Since "gayety" means a state of happiness, of course I do. Seriously, though, I think you mean "gayness," and I approve of all lifestyles that are lived safely, responsibly and take human rights into account. But it isn't really for me or you to approve or disapprove of anyone else's choice. People who pass severe judgment on anything but heterosexuality are usually very fearful and may be worried about their own sexual orientation. It's not up to you to judge someone else's sexual

166

orientation. In growing up, and getting to know yourself, you make the choice about your own life and then let others do what they want, as long as there is caring and respect.

Q: When a girl is sick and has sex with another girl, will they have a baby?
A: No. Babies result only from a combination of sperm from a male and eggs from a female. But, more importantly, girls who make love with other girls—lesbians—are not sick. They're just different from girls who make love with guys.

Q: Why are so many people gay?
A: Because gayness (either homosexual or bisexual) is a normal human behavior. Lack of this knowledge is the reason there is such a high incidence of suicide among teens who may experience sexual feelings for members of their own sex. With better education, such tragedies can be prevented.

Q: Is homosexuality a serious mental illness?
A: It's not a mental illness at all. In fact, the American Psychiatric Association took homosexuality off their list of mental illnesses. Homosexuality is a perfectly normal human behavior. Many human beings have the capacity to be turned on by both sexes or either sex. I call this "omnisexuality."

Q: Do all gays have anal sex?
A: No. In fact, a recent study has shown that the favorite sexual activity among gay men is oral sex. Then comes manual sex (mutual masturbation), with anal sex coming in third. What's more, it's a myth that *only* homosexual and bisexual men practice anal sex. Another study found that approximately 30 percent of heterosexually active teenagers practice anal sex as a contraceptive measure. Don't forget, in the quest for pleasure, people will try anything sexual and many people really find anal sex very exciting. Of course, as with all techniques, we need to practice them safely and respectfully.

Q: I'm worried. I think my kid brother (he's 16) is gay. He goes out with girls and has sex with them, but he acts more turned on when he's with certain guys. How can I tell?
A: It may be that your brother is bisexual and can enjoy sexual activity with both males and females. Maybe, on the Hacker Continuum, he majors in homosexuality and minors in hetersexuality. As he grows up and explores different relationships (I hope safely, respectfully, and caringly), he will eventually discover what his orientation is. I hope, though, that he won't suffer from an identity crisis, as too many kids do. Instead of worrying about him, perhaps you can influence him to seek out a support group which

will help him come to terms with his sexual orientation.

Q: I heard you say that all sex styles are normal. How do you know?
A: It's important to examine the evidence that exists from many disciplines. To give just a few examples, a number of reliable historical sources report that in ancient Greece, numerous important men who had wives and children also had male lovers. Anthropology also tells us that in some cultures a person with homosexual or bisexual tendencies is placed in a position of honor, often being the lover of a chief. All through history, privileged men in many different cultures were allowed to have male lovers. Recent research has indicated that among identical twins, if one twin identifies himself or herself as a homosexual, in 52 percent of the cases the other does as well. I've been asked why it isn't 100 percent among identical twins. It's highly likely that many of them fall somewhere toward the middle of my continuum; and although they might major in homosexuality, to one degree or another, one of them might choose to identify as a heterosexual.

Q: Doesn't the Bible teach that being gay is wrong?
A: The Bible considers lying down with another man an abomination. It also teaches that the

spilling of one's seed on the ground (i.e., outside a vagina) is a sin. In other words, anything that didn't lead to the possibility of reproduction in those ancient times, when the Bible was written, and when survival was so important, was seen as evil.

The Bible is a remarkable book, and many of its valuable teachings are still relevant today. But we must always consider the time in which it was written and realize that many of the biblical tenets which were true thousands of years ago are no longer as relevant. For example, we generally don't sacrifice animals, make burnt offerings, exclude women from certain religious practices, or adhere to food restrictions anymore. What's more, there are numerous interpretations of the Bible—whole churches are built on these different interpretations, and different sects within the various churches don't always agree. Interpretations of the Scriptures are always changing as times change. In the eighteenth century, the Roman Catholic church accepted abortion up to 40 days after conception, the point at which it believed the soul entered the body. Later, as times and Church leadership changed, abortion became unacceptable, as it remains today.

When it comes to homosexuality, many churches within a number of major religions conduct homosexual unions: a formal ceremony between same-sex people equivalent to marriage. And there are even gay ministers and priests.

Biblical passages have always been used selectively to support someone's particular point of view. There are many people who use the Bible for their own narrow purposes and refuse to stop, learn and think. Here's the perfect example of nonthinking:

A woman, on hearing about topless bars, declared angrily, "If God had meant us to run around nude, we would have been born that way!"

That's why we need to look also at other teachings, research and philosophies in order to arrive at an informed judgment.

Q: I come from a moral Christian home, and I think homosexuality is sick. So how can I agree with you?

A: When Anita Bryant was at the height of her gay-bashing campaign, she was reported to have said, "If God had meant there to be homosexuals, He would have created Adam and Bruce." Now, this may be funny, but consider this: If someone were to say "If God had meant blacks to be equal He would have created Adam and Sheba," you might call that person a bigot. By the same token, Anita Bryant is a bigot.

I don't ask people to adopt my values, nor do I want to be pressured to adopt theirs. All I ask, when people state their values, is "Based on what?" If people would engage in an ongoing, reasoned process of examining the basis for their values, they would then realize that, with knowledge gleaned from all disciplines, including the Bible, it is possible to reach varying conclusions. When we can defend our values with evidence, then we can learn to listen to each other's points of view. Only then can we realize that no one value is the absolute right one.

Q: Can gay people have children?
A: Yes, they can, but whether they will or not is up to them. People who are exclusively homosexual are not attracted to people of the opposite sex and so might not have children. However, many same-sex couples are now having families either by adoption or, in the case of lesbians, donor insemination. People who are not exclusively homosexual but major in homosexuality and minor in heterosexuality might very well marry and have children, since they can enjoy sexual activity with people of either gender.

It's important to know that kids raised by gay and lesbian couples do not automatically grow up to be gay, just as kids raised by heterosexual couples don't necessarily grow up to be heterosexual.

Q: If you look at male and female anatomy, you can see that they are made to be with each other. It's natural, so how can you say it's normal for same-sex couples to be together?
A: That is true if you maintain that sexuality is for procreation only. From all the knowledge we

have gained in the numerous years since the Bible was written with its focus on procreation, we now know that we also evolved as pleasure-seeking organisms. As you will find stated elsewhere in this book, we satisfy our pleasures in numerous ways. It was very clever of evolution to build in the drive to achieve sexual pleasure because somewhere in all of it, there will be enough vaginal intercourse to ensure procreation. But that doesn't mean that other ways are not normal or natural. I am not saying that we should engage in unbridled, unrestrained pleasuring. My consistent message is that it must be pursued only with safety and responsibility, and that appropriate limits need to be learned and practiced.

Chapter 12
What about Incest, Rape, and Sexual Harassment?

While we acknowledge a wide variety of normal sexual behaviors, certain sexual practices are simply not acceptable because they are nonconsensual (not agreed to by both people) and exploitive. These include incest, rape, and sexual harassment.

Incest is having sex with a member of your immediate family. While sexual *feelings* toward your family members are perfectly normal, *acting* on them is not appropriate because it is not an *grown-up* thing to do. The practice of incest has long been a taboo in almost every culture. Once you know the history, it's not hard to understand why.

Early in human evolution, we discovered that incest caused rivalries and disruption in family groups. This was, of course, dangerous in times when cohesive groups were essential to survival because, without each other, the group would die of exposure to the elements, lack of food, or attack by wild creatures. What's more, it is possible that inbreeding can cause a weakening of the gene pool that might produce sickly offspring.

It's true that in some societies, allowances were made for incest, but it was mostly among the ruling class. For example, in Ancient Egypt and Hawaii, royalty was permitted to wed only brother or sister, presumably to maintain purity in the royal line. But for the most part, incest has been taboo pretty much everywhere.

It is estimated that two-thirds of all incest cases are perpetrated by fathers, grandfathers or father figures. When a man has an erotic thought about his daughter or granddaughter *and acts on it,* he shows no self-discipline and often regards these women as property to be used as he sees fit. When incest occurs with a child, it is the ultimate betrayal, because kids depend on adults to take care of them, and they are at the mercy of the adults. One of the most damaging results of incest is the tendency on the part of the girl to blame herself for her father's or grandfather's actions.

A growing number of cases of boys being sexually abused by adult male family members has been discovered as well. Boys are often sodomized, which means being penetrated orally or anally. What's more unfortunate, a number of mothers will deny that such activity is occurring in order to protect their husbands and their marriages. These women may be dependent and intimidated enough so that they do not report the sexual abuse to anyone.

Rape is another unacceptable sexual behavior. Rape means that sexual relations are forced on one of the parties involved. Most rape cases involve men and women but many involve men and other men, and men and boys. Whether or not both parties are initially aroused by each other, if one asks the other to stop at any point, that request must be respected. If it isn't, that's rape.

The incidence of date and acquaintance rape is on the rise in this country. That might be due to a certain sense of entitlement that men still have left over from the old norm I wrote about earlier. These men, being in a position of power, feel that they deserve to be satisfied if they became sexually aroused. As a result, when men like these meet a girl and the two of them get sexually turned on by each other and start "fooling around," if the girl should say she doesn't want to go all the way for whatever reason, very often, the guy will get angry and force her to have intercourse against her wishes. His only focus is his erection and his feeling that he must resolve it by penetrating her vagina. This is not acceptable. No guy ever died of an unresolved erection. It will go away, and it will definitely come back when he is aroused again! What's more, any erection can be resolved by solo masturbation or by mutual masturbation, if that is agreeable to both partners.

A recent, very important study, sheds further light on the issue of date and acquaintance rape. Males and females apparently have different perceptions of what "agreement" to sex means. When a girl shows interest in kissing, caressing, and even necking and petting, a boy may misinterpret her behavior to mean that she is interested in sexual intercourse. When a girl says no, it is very often seen by boys as "maybe"—the beginning of a bargaining process in which he uses stronger and stronger persuasion until she says yes. The sad part is that, if a woman says no several times and the guy refuses to take her seriously, she may eventually believe that her refusals are ineffectual and she can do nothing but give in.

This is all a leftover of the old norm, when

women were supposed to say no even if they meant yes. This game playing is still going on, although many women are beginning to realize that they need to really mean it when they say no. Because we are still caught between two norms, date or acquaintance rape is a consequence of the inconsistency with which males and females are socialized in this society and can logically be viewed as one possible outcome of the male-aggressive, female-passive behavioral messages learned from childhood on. We must begin to change early sex-role socialization to avoid the kind of miscommunication and coercion patterns that too often crop up in later dating relationships.

Stranger rape is not motivated by the naturally occurring sexual needs that are experienced by most people. While date rape is usually associated with sexual drives, stranger rape is simply an aggressive and violent abuse of power.

Sexual harassment is harder to define because the definition changes rapidly and encompasses a wide range of behaviors from verbal expression to physical expression. Not so long ago, if a man called a woman "sweetie," or told an off-color joke in her presence, it was not considered a terrible thing. These days, it might constitute sexual harassment. We may be carrying things too far.

The key point to remember about incest, rape, and sexual harassment is that each has an element of exploitation, and that is what makes it unacceptable. Sex and sexuality are normal and can be a wonderful part of our lives as human beings, but only if both parties want it equally.

Here are some questions kids have asked me about incest, rape, and sexual harassment:

Q: Is it OK to parade a new dress or a bathing suit in front of your father?

A: It *should* be OK! I'm guessing, though, that the reason you are asking this question is that you got the idea, perhaps from your father, that when you wore certain clothes, you aroused him, and it was your fault for arousing him. A person who has grown up and is an adult can certainly have sexual feelings, thoughts, and fantasies, even for family members, but does not act on them in inappropriate situations. Incest is a nonadult behavior and is always inappropriate. However, you should be aware that provocative actions can cause a reaction. It is definitely not your fault if you turn someone on by the clothes you wear. It is the other person's responsibility to own up to his feelings and recognize what's OK to act on and what isn't.

Q: How should you handle molestation by a family member?

A: First say no very firmly! If that family member ignores you when you refuse to engage in any sexual activity with him/her, find someone you trust, like a teacher, counselor, relative, or friend of the family, and ask that person to help you. "Adults" in a family who exploit a child, need to get therapy so they can learn to grow up. There are agencies in every community which can be of help.

Q: I was raped. Why do I feel it was my fault it happened?
A: We still have that lingering feeling in our society that men can't control themselves. Therefore, if they rape a woman, it must be that she wore something or did something to arouse him. Not true! Grown-up men can control themselves and, if they don't, they never learned how to be an adult. Try to get some counseling so you can learn that it was not your fault!

Q: How long does it take for someone to get over their past if they were a rape and incest victim?
A: A lot depends on the particular incident. If it was brutal, or if a knife or gun were used, it's pretty frightening, and stays in a person's memory for a long time. Also, when a person is raped by a member of his or her family, especially when he or she is told that harm will occur if the act is revealed to anyone, it represents such a betrayal of trust that it may affect the victim for a very long time. If you seek out good counseling, however, and come to realize that it wasn't your fault and that you are not sullied for life, you can heal.

We also need to recognize that being sexually abused is only one way that people exploit each other. It should not be interpreted as being the dirtiest, most horrible abuse that can happen to anyone. There is NO question that it is an awful, hateful thing to have happen, but, in our society, tainted with shame, guilt and dirtiness about sexuality, the horror of the abuse is sometimes so exaggerated that it takes even longer to heal than it really needs to.

Q: Is forced sex by someone illegal?
A: Yes, it is rape. Different states in this country have different criteria for the definition of rape, but no one has the right to force anyone to engage in any kind of sexual activity.

Q: Do you think males can be sexually harassed by females, as well as vice versa?
A: Yes, of course. Anyone who persists in teasing, making sexual remarks, touching, telling dirty jokes, and so forth after it is made clear that such behavior is unwelcome, is guilty of sexual harassment. Although there has been change recently, it is still more prevalent for males to engage in this kind of behavior. There are, however, some reports that women who achieve economic power may, if they haven't grown up, act a great deal like some men and occasionally make sexual demands of their employees.

Q: What about psychological abuse in a relationship?

A: A young girl once said to me, "My boyfriend says he loves me but he's always putting me down."

And I said, "That's not love, because people who love you never demean you. They respect you and are your friend." If you have self-esteem, you don't allow yourself to be treated in an abusive way nor do you treat someone else abusively.

Q: Why do some young girls accept sexual harassment as "normal" or "expected"?

A: This is a holdover from the old days, when men had a great deal more economic power than women. Women were not encouraged to develop themselves fully or to become educated for a career. They were just supposed to be obedient wives. Therefore, many women depended on marriage for security and identity. As a result, men were seen as valuable commodities and often got away with a lot of disrespectful behavior toward women. And women often felt that it was normal to be treated in a less-than-respected way. Some of this double standard persists even today. We must begin to make young people realize how much better relationships can be and how much more pleasure could be derived if there were more equality between partners. This concept of equality extends to *all* relationships.

Q: What do you do when you have an abusive boyfriend?
A: If you want a real surge in self-esteem, just dump him! Why should you take that kind of treatment? I know it can be painful to lose a boyfriend but, as Sparky Anderson, coach of the Detroit Tigers, says to his team, "A little pain never hurt nobody!" In fact, pain can lead to growth and increased self-esteem. And the more you are willing to grow, the better your future relationships will be!

Q: Is date rape because the people are crazy or horny?
A: They are usually not crazy. Sometimes they're high on alcohol or drugs. They are usually horny, so they get into some kissing, necking, or petting. Quite often, however, the girl changes her mind because she gets scared of a possible pregnancy or a sexually transmitted disease. When that happens, she might try to stop the guy from going further—and she certainly has that right. It's perfectly normal for the guy to be disappointed or even angry. But he has *no* right to force her to have intercourse if she doesn't want to. If he's a responsible adult, he will tell her his feelings, but he will *never* rape her. If the two of them know about outercourse alternatives, they can pleasure each other in ways that exclude intercourse or they can engage in fantasy and friction (masturbation) when they are alone again.

Q: Why do they treat rape victims like criminals?
A: Because women used to be—and sometimes still are—blamed for being raped. However, things are changing. Many more men are now being imprisoned for rape, and fewer women are being blamed. Today's problem is that very few prisons have good rehabilitation programs to help rapists learn that what they did was an exploitive, nonadult thing. Often, when these men are released, they repeat the behavior. There are some programs around the country which offer a fairly long-term counseling opportunity for rehabilitation. In the case of incest, both the perpetrator and the family go into counseling for about 2 years. At some point, the male makes a pledge to everyone not to engage in this behavior again. He also continues the counseling visits under the supervision of a probation officer. The children who have been abused pledge not to exploit the situation and use guilt to get things they want. For example, they promise never to say, "After what you did to me, you mean you won't give me the keys to the car?"

Q: Why do people rape other people?
A: There are a couple of reasons. In the case of stranger rape, it's more a matter of power and violence than sexuality. A person who has problems relating to others or who is full of hate will take out those very hostile feelings by pouncing on someone unexpectedly and molesting that per-

son. Date or acquaintance rape is sexually motivated, and the perpetrator simply doesn't know how to control his sexual impulses if he is frustrated. In other words, he hasn't grown up.

Q: When women say no to sex, do they really mean it? Or do they want us guys to convince them to do it?
A: Guys have to treat all nos seriously. Even if a girl is not sure, she certainly will not enjoy being pressured. It's so much better to slow down and let both your sexual desires build gradually.

Q: When I was growing up, all I learned was to get all you can. How can I ever change?
A: It might not be easy to break out of your mind set, but you can do it. Think of it as your opportunity to become a great lover and, more importantly, to create a good, enduring relationship with someone. All the research shows that people who do a lot of bed hopping with lots of partners enjoy sex less and put themselves at the greatest risk of contracting STDs. Learn some of the principles this book is trying to teach, and turn over a new leaf!

Chapter 13
What about Dealing with Your Parents?

Teens have been sexual ever since teens have been around. And teens have hidden their sexuality for that long, too. Dealing with your parents is one area that really needs to be examined.

The first thing you have to understand is that

your parents are interested in what you're doing because they love you. And, these days, there's good reason for parents to be worried—intercourse is much more prevalent and much more dangerous than it was when they were teens. At that time, the rules were different. When teens "sneaked" around, it consisted mainly of necking and petting. Everyone went home with congested pelvises. The boys called it "blue balls" and, I suppose, you could say the girls had "pink pelvis." Today, however, no one thinks it's necessary to delay gratification, so sexual intercourse often happens very early in a relationship.

Since we haven't been taught how to handle this change in behavior, there are an awful lot of unintended pregnancies and sexually transmitted diseases being passed around out there. It's not difficult to understand why parents worry. The trouble is parents haven't been educated either. That's why a lot of the worry comes out as preaching, pestering, and even punishing you.

Many kids tell me, "You know how teenagers are. If someone tells you not to do something, you're just gonna do it!" That's pretty normal teen behavior. And it's knowing this teen characteristic that causes parents to feel concerned. So, at the same time as we make an effort to educate parents, teens everywhere need to jump in and show their moms and dads that they can act responsibly and take care of themselves.

Here are few tips on how to help your parents ease into your dating years:

• Demonstrate that you can be responsible in other areas.

If you're asked to do household chores, to fix your bike, to take care of a younger brother or sister, or to do your homework, try to be consistent and carry out these tasks.

• Point out to your parents often how well you're doing and how responsible and reliable you are. That will build trust between you and your folks. Then, when you start dating and having relationships of different kinds, you can remind them how trustworthy you have been in the past. This will encourage them to continue to trust you.

• Be as honest as possible with your folks. Don't lie to them about where you're going, where you've been, or who you've been with. The more honest you can be, the less reason your parents will have to suspect you.

• Tell your folks what you're doing to take care of yourself sexually. Make sure they know that you're not acting irresponsibly. Make sure they know you're taking every precaution to protect yourself from unwanted pregnancies and sexually transmitted diseases.

• If your folks really object to what you're doing, explain patiently to them that this is what you're doing, and that you're doing it as safely, responsibly and risk-free as possible. Try to make them understand that it's better to do it your way than to sneak around and take chances with your health and the health of your partner.

• Don't be discouraged. If your folks get angry or disapprove or ground you, at least you know you've been honest with them.

• Always carry a new condom. It's the safest contraceptive around.

• Educate your parents. If you can, bring home information about things you've learned in school or from books. Try to persuade your parents and siblings to read or discuss these things with you. I know that some kids have parents who are not always willing to talk about sexuality. If you've really tried and they continue to resist, it might be a good idea to find a counselor or teacher you like, or even an older friend or relative, with whom you can discuss these things.

• Whatever you do, don't try to get even with your parents. This can cause you to do things that will put you and your partner at risk. Think of your own health first and gather information so you can continue to grow up safe and healthy and have fun exploring pleasuring the rest of your life.

SUGGESTED READINGS

Alyson, S. et al. *Young, Gay and Proud!* Boston: Alyson, 1981.

Berzon, B. (Ed.). *Positively Gay.* Los Angeles: Mediamix Association, 1984.

Blume, Judy. Any of her novels for young adults.

Boston Women's Health Collective. *The New Our Bodies, Ourselves.* New York: Simon & Schuster, 1992.

Cassell, C. *Swept Away—Why Women Fear Their Own Sexuality.* New York: Bantam, 1985.

Ford, M. T. *100 Questions and Answers About AIDS: What You Need to Know Now.* New York: Beech Tree Books, 1993.

Gale, J. *A Young Man's Guide to Sex.* New York: Holt, Rinehart & Winston, 1984.

Gordon, S. and Gordon, J. *Raising a Child Conservatively in a Sexually Permissive World.* New York: Simon & Schuster, 1986.

Gordon, S. and Dickman, I. *Schools and Parents: Partners in Sex Education.* Public Affairs Pamphlet #581. Public Affairs Committee, 381 Park Avenue South, New York, NY 10016, 1988.

Gordon, S. *Seduction Lines Heard 'Round the World and Answers You Can Give.* New York: Prometheus, 1987.

Gordon, S. *The Teenage Survival Book.* New York: Times Books, 1991.

Gordon, S. *Why Love Is Not Enough.* Boston: Bob Adams, Inc., 1988.

Hamilton, Eleanor. *Sex with Love.* Boston: Beacon Press, 1978.

Hass, A. *Teenage Sexuality.* New York: Pinnacle Books, 1981.

Heron, Ann (Ed.). *One Teenager in Ten: Testimonies by Gay and Lesbian Youth.* New York: Warner, 1983.

HMI. *Tales from the Closet* (Comic Book Series). New York: Hetrick-Martin Institute, 1991. $1.25 each. Call (212) 633-8920.

Klein, M. *Ask Me Anything.* New York: Simon & Schuster, 1992.

Leight, I. *Raising Sexually Healthy Children.* New York: Avon, 1990.

McCarthy, B. and McCarthy, E. *Sexual Awareness: Enhancing Sexual Pleasure.* New York: Carroll & Graf Publishers, Inc., 1984.

McNaught, B. *A Disturbed Peace.* Washington, DC: Dignity Press, 1981.

McNaught, B. *On Being Gay.* New York: St. Martin's Press, 1986.

Planned Parenthood. *How to Talk with Your Child About Sexuality.* New York: Doubleday, 1988.

Voss, J. and Gale, J. *A Young Woman's Guide to Sex.* New York: Henry Holt, 1984.